OVERHEARD
IN DUBLIN
RIDES AGAIN

DUBLIN WIT FROM
OVERHEARDINDUBLIN.COM

OVERHEARD IN DUBLIN RIDES AGAIN

DUBLIN WIT FROM
OVERHEARDINDUBLIN.COM

Gill & Macmillan

Gill & Macmillan Ltd
Hume Avenue, Park West, Dublin 12
with associated companies throughout the world
www.gillmacmillan.ie
© Gerard Kelly and Sinéad Kelly 2010
978 07171 45416

Print origination by TypeIT, Dublin
Illustrations by Eoin Coveney
Printed in the UK by CPI Cox & Wyman

This book is typeset in 10pt Garamond Book on 11pt.

The paper used in this book comes from the wood pulp
of managed forests. For every tree felled, at least one
tree is planted, thereby renewing natural resources.

A CIP catalogue record for this book is available from
the British Library

5 4 3 2 1

Polski?

I was recently in a hair salon where I overheard a hairdresser talking to a tanned girl whose hair she was blow-drying.

Hairdresser: 'So girl, where ya from?'

Girl: 'Iran.'

Hairdresser: 'Ukraine? Jaysus, really? But, like, you don't look Polish at all!'

Cue silence from the girl who didn't have a clue what was going on.

Overheard by Anonymous, Peter Mark
Posted on Friday, 26 March 2010

Oh yeah?

On the one and only occasion there was an e-voting machine in the local voting station due to a referendum of some sort. One of the neighbours met me on her way out and proceeded to explain the e-voting process. Having gone through all the nitty-gritty she finishes up with:

'... and when you've all that done, you just press 'NO'.

Overheard by Anonymous, outside the local polling station
Posted on Tuesday, 23 March 2010

Muppet on the train

Travelling from Holyhead on the train with a group of lads from Dublin. Out across the countryside and far off distant mountains, one guy sees a very remote little house, turns to the other guy and says,

'Jaysus, will you look at that gaff out there in the middle of nowhere, who would want to live out there?'

The other guy answers, 'Probably some hermit.' Then, noticing the confused look on the first guy's face asks, 'You know what a hermit is, don't you?'

'Yeah, of course I do,' the first guy answers confidently, 'it's a frog.'

Overheard by P, on the Holyhead to Manchester train
Posted on Tuesday, 23 March 2010

Looking at the chimps

Family day out in Dublin Zoo, at the chimpanzee enclosure, guy beside us showing his children the chimps.

'Ah jaysus, I though' dat was his face, it's his arse!'

Cue looks from assembled parents ... 'Eh, sorry, bum,' he says.

Overheard by F, Dublin Zoo

Posted on Wednesday, 17 March 2010

Seachtain na Gaeilge in action

An Eastern European beggar at Abbey Street Luas station appeared to be having an argument with a well-dressed man, who promptly stormed off.

A young Dublin lad who witnessed this shouts after the man, 'You're one bleeding amadán!'

Overheard by I, Abbey Street

Posted on Monday, 15th March 2010

Biro, the Irish for pen

I was in Supermac's on O'Connell Street at the till when a man, who was either drugged up or drunk, came up to the counter and cut ahead of me to say 'give me a Biro' to the Eastern European girl who was serving, to which she looked confused as the man slurred his words in a thick Dublin accent. He said 'give me a Biro' a few more times until the manager interceded and gave him a pen. As he was about to walk away he turned to the girl and waved the pen and said:

'Biro is the Irish for pen, love!'

Overheard by M, Supermac's, O'Connell Street

Posted on Friday, 12 March 2010

Cash, card or Mars bar? The new payment method!

A very drunk man was getting on the bus and wouldn't pay the fare. He said he only wanted to go two stops down the road and he had no change. The driver refused and the man then handed over a Mars bar! Considering this to be adequate form of payment, he went to take a seat. The driver got out, escorted him off the bus yelling, 'Ye can keep ur bleedin' Mars bar!' Perhaps he was more of a Snickers fan ...

Overheard by S, no. 27 bus
Posted on Wednesday, 10 March 2010

Couldn't see him!

Sitting on the bus, listening to an elderly woman in deep conversation with her daughter. She was venting her frustrations at how her movie night in had been ruined by some 'feckin' eejit down the corner of the screen waving his arms all over the place' during the black and white movie she'd recorded. Her daughter tried to explain that it was more than likely just the sign-language narrator they use for the deaf. I really had to hold in the giggles though when the elderly lady said:

'But sure Jane Wyman couldn't even see him when she was walking by!'

Overheard by Christina, bus into town
Posted on Friday, 5 March 2010

Slight word mix-up!!

On a taxi out of town the other day, passed by the Olympia theatre and noticed a group of teenagers hanging around outside all dressed in Goth gear. On seeing this the taxi driver (lovely old-timer) commented:

'Jays wud ya luk at them dressed up like dat, sure I suppose dere only young and da haemorrhoids are at them!'

I hadn't the heart to correct him and suggest that maybe he meant hormones.

Overheard by Ciaran, Dame Street
Posted on Tuesday, 2 March 2010

Anyone seen a tiger?

Friend of mine on jury duty for a tiger kidnapping trial. Sitting in the local one night, everybody quizzing him and him giving nothing away, when one of the girls says, 'Can you even tell us where they kidnapped the tiger from?'

Overheard by Larry, the local
Posted on Sunday, 28 February 2010

Mary Coughlan

Taxi driver complaining about Tánaiste Mary Coughlan:

'I didn't like her when she sung either!'

Overheard by Anonymous, taxi in Dublin
Posted on Saturday, 27 February 2010

Predictable but still funny

Two girls chatting.

1st girl: 'Me da is gettin' a terrible belly on him.'

2nd girl: 'Maybe it's in the genes?'

1st girl: 'No, it's in every trousers he wears.'

Overheard by Aimee, Stephen's Green Park bench
Posted on Monday, 25 January 2010

Ya gotta love Dublin Bus drivers

Today I was getting on the no. 145 bus into town. A French guy was in front of me. He asks the bus driver: 'Does this bus go near Pembroke Road?'

Bus driver replies: 'You're better off getting no. 45, it'll bring you closer.'

French guy: 'Do you know when that bus will be here?'

Bus driver: 'I don't know, I can only drive one bus at a time.'

Gotta love Dublin Bus drivers.

Overheard by Anonymous, Loughlinstown
Posted on Thursday, 25 February 2010

Out of order

One night I was out with a friend of mine from Kildare, who told me a story of when he was in a lock-in at a pub in Leixlip when the gardaí raided it. All the people in this pub were hiding in the gents'. The two gardaí walked into the gents', one started taking names of the punters, the other started kicking open the cubicle doors. When he came to the last one it was locked, only a voice of a drunk man could be heard shouting: 'THIS TOILET IS OUT OF ORDER.'

Overheard by Anonymous, somewhere in Leixlip
Posted on Thursday, 25 February 2010

No meat

We were in the Bad Ass restaurant in Temple Bar. My daughter is a vegetarian. We ordered meat dishes to which my five-year-old son shouted out 'but Ma! Laura is a virgin!' to a stunned waiter.

Overheard by Brendan, Bad Ass cafe
Posted on Tuesday, 23 February 2010

Search everywhere?

Real Dub head at departures in Dublin Airport at 11.30 in the morning, talking to two female airport workers, who were trying to locate his missing partner to get a flight boarded:

'Have you searched everywhere, she might have fallen asleep in de jax?'

Overheard by Eamo, Dublin Airport
Posted on Thursday, 18 February 2010

Make your own entertainment

I was on the Luas and there was a few minutes of a delay, due to a signalling fault. Aul' lad, obviously a bit worse for wear, trying to 'entertain' everyone kept saying to all those around him, including me, 'C'mon, give us a song ... I thought all you young ones were mad for the singing, do yis not all be watching Max Factor every Saturday, I love it.' Cue much giggling and laughing around him. Then the Luas moves off, and he says loudly, 'Ah, it's the

X factor I mean, that Max Factor, sure that's a woman's perfume!!!!'

Kept us all laughing during the delay ...

Overheard by Linda, on the red line Luas
Posted on Monday, 15 February 2010

Red or white wine?

Sitting in the car in a car park with my three-year-old daughter, waiting for my sister to arrive in her car. I said to my daughter,

'Now, watch out for her, won't you?'

'Well, what colour is her car?'

'It's wine.'

'Red or white, Mammy?'

Overheard by Clodagh, Frascati Shopping Centre, Blackrock
Posted on Wednesday, 10 February 2010

Slip of the tongue

I overheard my sister talking to someone about her daughter, who was recovering in hospital. 'Yes, we got her out of the hospital and took her for a nice, long walk along the pier in Howth, and then dropped her back in.'

Overheard by Leo, Churchtown
Posted on Wednesday, 10 February 2010

What did you take?

Working one night in Bray Garda Station. Two prisoners are in the cells, one for drink-driving, the other for robbing a car. A doctor arrived to check out the drink-driver. When finished the Sergeant asked him to look at the other lad who

was off his head on drugs – yer man was out of it goofin' off. The doctor tried to bring him around saying, 'I'm a doctor, are you okay? What did you take? What did you take?'

The gauger came to and says, 'A Honda Civic.'

Overheard by tonzer, Bray Garda Station
Posted on Wednesday, 10 February 2010

Phone abuse

A woman in work on the phone to a disgruntled client.

'I'm sorry, sir, but I won't allow you to physically abuse me on the phone.'

Overheard by Dermot, Dublin 18
Posted on Tuesday, 9 February 2010

Belly-button decision

Sitting in an antenatal class and the midwife starts explaining about when the baby is born. She is going through how your partner is asked to cut the cord when a youngish Dublin girl interrupts her. She asks if this is when you can ask for an 'inny' or an 'outty' belly-button.

Needless to say the midwife has to check that

the girl is being serious. All of us other women have to try not to look at each other and hold in our giggles, as the girl defends herself saying she thought you could choose!

Overheard by Louise, antenatal class, Rotunda Hospital
Posted on Sunday, 31 January 2010

Aeroplane sightseeing

On a plane to Liverpool, bunch of young wans obviously on their first trip to the city. As we begin our descent into Liverpool airport one of girls behind us starts pointing out the window at all the 'cultural' landmarks she can see ('Jaysus Jacinta, look they have ASDA here!!'). Suddenly she starts shouting excitedly to her friend.

'Quick, look, look, it's Anfield stadium!!! I don't believe it, I'm actually looking at Anfield stadium!!!'

Her friend has a look out the window and the next thing we hear: 'That's a bleedin' roundabout ya gobshite!'

Overheard by Sheena, Ryanair flight to Liverpool
Posted on Wednesday, 27 January 2010

Globe trotters ...

I'm currently a student teacher. I recently had Senior Infants (5–6 year olds). I decided to teach Geography and to see what countries the children knew, so I asked them what countries in the world they could list. I got the usual countries, America, Spain, England, and so on. I decided to prompt the children into naming other countries. I asked 'can anyone tell me where pizza comes from?' hoping for the answer Italy. Instead, I was greeted with a young boy

waving his hand around desperately. His answer:
'Apache!'

Overheard by Mari, in class
Posted on Monday, 25 January 2010

Higher taxes

More seen than heard.

On a Tesco ad it said: 'Was 1.40 now 1.45'. I
think you can see the mistake.

Overheard by Anonymous, Crumlin Shopping Centre
Posted on Friday, 22 January 2010

That takes me back ...

I was at the third annual Legalise Cannabis
march in Dublin and we were all outside the
Dáil. Everyone was lighting up and the smoke
was starting to get thick when one of the gardaí
wandering through the crowd says to himself:
'Jaysus, that smell brings me back 20 years.'

You couldn't stop me from smiling all day!

Overheard by Bryan, Outside the Dáil
Posted on Thursday, 21 January 2010

Talked her way into that one

A couple of years ago I was in a queue in Pearse
Street Garda Station to get passport forms
signed. An aul' one in front of me was with her
granddaughter filling out forms for her stolen
purse. The child was bored and decided to
strike up a conversation with the garda.

Child: 'What's your name?'

Garda: 'Fiona'

Child: 'Oh, like princess Fiona in Shrek?'

Garda: 'Yeah, do you like Shrek? Maybe your Granny will take you to the pictures to see the new one?'

Child: 'Ah no. I've already seen it on DVD loads of times. Me Da has hundreds at home. He sells them ...'

Granny: 'Jesus, will yeh shut up?'

Other Garda: 'We won't have to drag you in for questioning, will we?'

Child looks at Granny with totally confused look on her face. Everyone in the queue and the two gardaí fell about the place laughing. The Granny seemed to get over her stolen purse pretty quickly and made her exit.

Overheard by Anonymous, Pearse Street Garda Station
Posted on Thursday, 21 January 2010

33N/1

On a Nitelink on the way home from a night out. Bus comes to a halt outside a bookmakers and the driver informs us that the bus has broken down. One lad on the phone to a mate says quite loudly, 'We're after breaking down outside Bambury bookmakers in Lusk ... what are the odds of that?'

Both levels of the bus went into hysterics.

Overheard by David, Lusk
Posted on Tuesday, 19 January 2010

The milk thieves

On the way home from college, two lads on the back of the bus were talking about their friend who was put in prison.

Lad #1: 'What did he get put in the 'joy for?'

Lad #2: 'He robbed the milkman, yeah he managed to get €300 and a carton of strawberry milk.'

Overheard by Rachel, on the no. 45a
Posted on Sunday, 17 January 2010

Mister cranky on the 39

Getting on a packed bus last week during one of the coldest days this winter. On the upper deck, a middle-aged woman gets on and opens one of the windows. The man sitting behind her immediately picks up his mobile and dials a number.

Man: 'Hi, how are you? Yeah? I'm sitting on the bus and if another person opens an effing window I'm gonna kill them right out! Okay, see you, bye.'

Cue strange looks from all passengers.

Overheard by Anonymous, no. 39 on Dame Street
Posted on Tuesday, 12 January 2010

Big ankles

Overheard a guy in a garage explaining to the mechanic that his car stopped in a puddle and when he got out he was 'up to his ankles in about three-feet of water'.

Overheard by Whalen, Statoil garage
Posted on Thursday, 7 January 2010

Tax-free

Sitting through a tourism movie-type thing in Collins Barracks that tried to persuade Americans in the 1930s, '40s and '50s to holiday in Ireland. An American man was the main character, as he was heading back through Shannon airport's off-licence, the narrator of the movie went something like this:

'Johnny has now bought his gifts for his loved ones back home, all tax-free, but he got the most important gift of all for himself, Kitty.' (This Irish girl he met.)

Before I could even blink, an aul' fella sitting behind me muttered to himself,

'Bet he didn't have to pay tax on her!'

I was in stitches desperately trying to hold back the laughter for the rest of the movie.

Overheard by Cillian, Collins Barracks
Posted on Wednesday, 6 January 2010

A case of the GHDs

There was this kid going absolutely bloody mental on the bus this morning ... his mother turned around to the woman next to her and said:

'I think he has a touch of dat GHD ting.'

The woman replied: 'I think you mean ADHT.'

To which the mother said, 'No, GHD the one that makes dem all hyper n'all, GHD it stands for somethin', hyper disease.'

Overheard by Anonymous, no. 122 bus
Posted on Monday, 4 January 2010

Trying to save time

Two lads in a queue for the cinema in front of me get to the desk, where one asks the cinema clerk,

'How long is Avatar, is it two hours?'

'No, it's three hours', replied the clerk.

'Three hours?!' He turns to the other lad and tells him in a horrified voice that it's three hours long. Then he turns back to the cinema clerk and asks him,

'How long is the 3D Avatar?'

Overheard by Ali, UCI Coolock
Posted on Thursday, 31 December 2009

Subtitles for Grannies

At my Gran's over Christmas, we were watching a documentary about Hitler. It was in German with English subtitles. My Granny, with her thick Dublin accent, takes the remote and starts turning up the volume.

'I can't bleedin' understand dem foreigners. Turn dat rite up til I hav a listen an see wat der sayin!'

I still don't think she had copped on to the subtitles.

Overheard by Tony, My Nan's house, Finglas
Posted on Tuesday, 29 December 2009

Fun at the beach

On Bray beach last week and a naked boy runs across the beach with his Ma and Da chasing him. The little boy shouts:

'I don't want the bird to eat me willie!'

His Da shouts back: 'We were only messing!'

Overheard by J.D., Bray beach
Posted on Monday, 28 December 2009

Spoonheads

I was on the Luas last August and was standing next to these two Cork guys.

Guy #1: 'Did you hear that some celebrity was stabbed yesterday?'

Guy #2: 'What? Who? What happened?'

Guy #1: 'Well, they were out with your woman Reese ... Reese ... Reese ... Whatsername?'

Guy #2: 'Witherspoon?'

Guy #1: 'With a spoon? No, with a knife! You can't stab someone wih a spoon!'

Overheard by Rachel, the Luas to Connolly Station
Posted on Saturday, 26 December 2009

Lost in Translation ... but we both speak English*

After being at an excellent Babyshambles gig where the surprise act at the end of the night

was Shane McGowan singing 'Dirty Old Town', I regaled my night's events to a friend.

'Went to see Babyshambles last night and you'll never guess who they pulled out of the bag at the end of the night ... only Shane McGowan!'

My friend smiled looking befuddled: 'No way, that's mad!'

Later on that day it must have been playing on her mind, because she questioned her colleague.

'My mate went to see Baby-something-or-other last night ... and they pulled Shane McGowan out of a bag? Did you hear about that?

Overheard by Anonymous, Dame Street
Posted on Friday, 18 December 2009

The kindness of strangers

Was in a Centra in town on my lunch break getting a roll. It was fairly busy and there was a big queue. There were two 'lads' in front of me getting a six-pack of Dutch and Devils Bit. One of them gestured for me to go in front of them in the queue. I said 'No thanks' and the other said 'Go on ahead mate, sure you have to be back in work in an hour, we're only to going to the f**king park!'

True gentlemen.

Overheard by David, Centra, Townsend Street
Posted on Sunday, 13 December 2009

Mouthing off

At home yesterday morning, chatting to my mother on the subject of snoring. She came out with this gem:

'Ahh, sure! I don't snore as much as I used to

since I got me nostrils removed when I was yer age.'

I think she meant to say tonsils! Had to bite my lip.

Overheard by McChubbin, at home in Swords
Posted on Monday, 14 December 2009

Annoying little brother

I was in Xtravision in Donaghmede and a harassed woman was there with a few kids. One boy was being particularly annoying to the little girl. Trying to take the boy to task she asks:

'Are you trying to tantalise your sister?'

I think she meant antagonise, bit of a difference there.

Overheard by Patricia, Xtravision, Donaghmede
Posted on Wednesday, 9 December 2009

Outfoxed

Coming home from working overseas some time ago I visited my sister, who had just had her fourth child – the oldest of which is six. My brother-in-law had brought a pup home for the kids and it was running round wagging its tail. The eldest asked my sister if the pup was going to have its tail foxed, whereupon my sister, looking up from feeding the latest her bottle, replied:

'No ... but your father is!'

Overheard by Frank, my sister's house in Coolock
Posted on Friday, 4 December 2009

How to economise during a recession!

The fashion commentator on RTE's *The Afternoon Show*, as a model was parading around the studio:

'... and, of course, with those shoes, you wouldn't need to wear much else ...'

Overheard by Anonymous, RTÉ One
Posted on Wednesday, 2 December 2009

Irish aural

In our Irish listening exam in summer, the examiner played the start of the CD to check for sound, she then said:

'Is that ok with everyone?'

To which one of the lads in the class shouts up:

'No, it's in f**king Irish.'

Whole class nearly wet themselves and the exam was delayed by five minutes!

Overheard by Rinnegan, in class
Posted on Monday, 30 November 2009

Whose hair is it anyway?

Class is studying *Romeo and Juliet*, the short version with pictures. They get to the picture of Juliet on the balcony and Romeo down below.

'I know this bit. Juliet, Juliet, let down your hair.'

'Don't be an eegit, that was Goldilocks.'

Overheard by Johnny, school in Terenure
Posted on Thursday, 26 November 2009

Expanding service

I've seen a sign on a takeaway stating 'Divers wanted'.

Must be the global warming.

Overheard by Kafebronz, North King Street
Posted on Tuesday, 24 November 2009

Getting on the 'Good' list Dublin-style!

In town last weekend, about to walk over the Ha'penny Bridge when Santa comes down the quays in a horse-drawn carriage, shouting 'Merry Christmas' – sleigh bells and everything. Two lads walking across the bridge spot him and one shouts:

'Santa ya legend!'

Definitely the Dublin way of getting onto his 'good' list!

Overheard by Bex, Ha'penny Bridge
Posted on Saturday, 21 November 2009

TD au naturel

Alan Shatter TD, speaking on the news, on RTE Radio 1 the other day. The presenter asks him a question, to which he begins to reply, but there's whiny feedback. The presenter cuts across Shatter, asking him if he has a radio on in the background that's causing the interference.

'No, I've nothing on at all,' replies Shatter.

I wonder does he do all his phone interviews naked?

Overheard by Anonymous, RTE Radio 1
Posted on Friday, 20 November 2009

The cheek!

While my Granddad was in hospital, we were waiting down the hall from his room while nurses tended to him. Around the corner, a conversation was going on between a doctor and a hospital volunteer.

Doctor: 'Well, Mary, how was the holiday?'

Mary: 'Oh, I didn't go after all. The mother went about dyin' on us the day before. Well, I was like an anti-Christ!'

Overheard by butterfly, hospital
Posted on Thursday, 19 November 2009

Sounds painful

One elderly lady telling another that her sister-in-law was 'ridiculed' with arthritis.

Overheard by Anonymous, no. 39 bus
Posted on Tuesday, 10 November 2009

A land far, far away

Our Economics lecturer was trying to illustrate the impact Ireland's imports have by using the toys kids ask for at Christmas as an example.

'Where do Playstations come from?'

'Japan,' we answer.

'What about the Wii?'

'Japan.'

'Ok, what about Lego?'

Brief pause and some wagon says, 'Legoland?'

Overheard by ac, ITT Dublin, Tallaght
Posted on Wednesday, 4 November 2009

Pizza

Sitting at home doing the usual Friday night take-away orders, my mother yells at the computer at which she was searching Pizza Delivery services on:

'I don't want Italian! I want f**king pizza!'

Overheard by Leanne & Robyn, my living room
Posted on Friday, 23 October 2009

Bored little girl's breakthrough idea

At mass a very bored little girl said:

'Why don't they just shoot the devil?'

Overheard by Justine, Dalkey mass
Posted on Friday, 23 October 2009

Universal appeal

In Religion class a few weeks ago. The teacher asks us to think of someone really interesting, someone we wouldn't mind being locked in a train compartment with for six hours. Going around the class, people are saying Nelson Mandela, their dad, whoever.

She gets to me and I say Colin Farrell, because he's had an interesting life, what with the drug problems, being a movie star, etc.

Teacher replies: 'I'll tell you now, if I was stuck on a train with Colin Farrell for six hours, talking would be one thing we wouldn't do!'

Cue slightly nervous laughter from the class.

Overheard by F, Religion class
Posted on Sunday, 18 October 2009

Community care

For our transition year community care myself and a friend were in the Capuchin Day Centre for the homeless and one day my friend was having a conversation with one of the visitors.

Visitor: 'So, why are you here then?'

Friend: 'We're on community care.'

Visitor: 'Ah, jaysus wha' did you do?'

Think she might have misunderstood community care for community service ...

Overheard by Rebecca, Capuchin Day Centre
Posted on Wednesday, 14 October 2009

Never trust a quiet kid!

I decided to bring my children to mass one Sunday. On the way I explained to my four-year-old that church is where God and Jesus lives and we were going to go and pray to them. I stressed how important it was to be quiet. My son was looking all around him when we arrived and I was surprised how well behaved he was, when all of a sudden at the top of his lungs he shouts:

'If this is God's house, where's the kitchen?'

Overheard by Andrea, Donnycarney Church
Posted on Wednesday, 14 October 2009

Gaelscoil

My nephew came home from his first day at Gaelscoil. His mam says,

'Did you like it? What's your teacher like?'

David, aged four, answers, 'She's great. She speaks English in two languages.'

Overheard by Anonymous, Edenmore, Dublin
Posted on Saturday, 3 October 2009

A funny thing happened on the way to Croker ...

My fiancé and I were heading to Croke Park to watch a hurling match. He was wearing a Wexford jersey and I was wearing a yellow bellies shirt. We were strolling by Trinity when a taxi driver said:

'Hey, marry that girl and make some more Wexford hurlers!'

Overheard by Angie, Grafton Street by Trinity College
Posted on Wednesday, 30 September 2009

The bus stop comedian

Standing waiting for a bus on Swords main street, when a Chinese bloke walks out of the local Chinese takeaway with a shopping trolley and two gas cylinders in it. An aul' fella also at the bus stop turns and shouts at him:

'Jaysus, you're a gas man!'

The Chinese man walks on looking very confused.

Overheard by j, Swords main street
Posted on Monday, 28 September 2009

Who says the public sector is a waste of money

Was on the DART coming home from Howth last summer when the train stopped just after Howth Junction. After five minutes the driver came on the PA in a heavy Dublin accent:

'The train will be delayed as Killester has gone on strike AGAIN!! Ahem ... Iarnród Éireann would like to apologise for any inconvenience caused.'

Overheard by Fifi, on the DART
Posted on Friday, 25 September 2009

Ryanair's new marketing tool

I was flying back from London recently. When we landed the steward was making the usual landing announcement over the intercom and finished with:

'If you've enjoyed your flight with us, please tell your friends, if not, tell them you flew with another airline.'

Overheard by Jo, Ryanair flight from Stansted to Dublin
Posted on Thursday, 24 September 2009

Fetish cheese

Male teenager #1: 'That Lisa one is bleedin' addicted to shoes, she has millions of them, it's like a fetish or something.'

Male teenager #2: 'Fetish? That's a cheese ya bleedin' eejit!'

Argument ensues!

Overheard by Orla, outside Peter's Pub on South William Street
Posted on Wednesday, 9 September 2009

Not exactly loving Tescos

Standing at the queue in Tesco and a guy asks for a bag to pack his groceries. The girl said they had no plastic bags as there was a shipment error, all they had were the one euro ones with Tesco written on the side.

'Jaysus Christ, this is worse than robbery, a bleedin' euro for a poxy bag and I have to pay you to advertise your bags?!'

His pulse was beginning to race and he was getting agitated as all his stuff was scanned and he needed at least two bags to carry it all.

Guy: 'I don't believe this, give me two.'

Girl: 'Thanks, do you have a club card?'

Guy: 'No.'

Girl: 'Would you like one?'

Guy: 'I'm not joining any f**ken club that charges one euro for a bleedin' carrier bag.'

Overheard by Tom, Tesco in Tallaght
Posted on Wednesday, 9 September 2009

Electric love

Walking past a tent at Electric Picnic in the early hours of Saturday morning, a lad in his early twenties emerges from a tent, having got lucky the night before. His female friend emerges after him and asks,

'So ... will I see you later then?'

To which he replies, 'Eh ... sure I'll find ya on Facebook.'

And swiftly exits the area to a roar of laughter around him!

Overheard by EP, Electric Picnic
Posted on Wednesday, 9 September 2009

Gotta know the lingo!

You know how teachers get kids to rest their heads on their folded arms on the desks and tell them:

'Heads down, téigh a codladh.'

Well, when I worked in a playschool, there was a wee English boy and he repeated:

'Heads down, take cover!'

He left soon after, obviously traumatised by the order.

Overheard by Turquoise, while working in a playschool
Posted on Friday, 4 September 2009

Strange offer

Not so much heard as seen.

Was on the no. 77 bus home when it pulled in at the stop on Kevin Street beside the newsagent. Sign in the window says: 'Great offer – buy a bar of Dove soap and get a jar of Uncle Ben's free!' Does anyone else see the connection?

Overheard by Laura, Kevin Street
Posted on Friday, 4 September 2009

Over-herd

I was on the no. 44 bus which passed a field with a few cows that still had their horns. A few seats up from me were two lads. After we past the field one turns, with great surprise, and mumbles something to the other. He in turn mumbles something back. This continues a few times until the second lad exclaims loudly:

'It's not a bleedin' antelope!'

Overheard by S, no. 44 bus
Posted on Tuesday, 1 September 2009

Tiger Woods

In the American Embassy, during the signing of the book of condolences for Senator Ted Kennedy, a stroppy teenager and his mother are next in line. The teenager points to a photo of President Barack Obama, and in all seriousness loudly declares:

'Why the hell is there a photo of Tiger Woods on the wall under President ...'

Needless to say he got a few dirty looks off the American staff.

Overheard by Anonymous, American Embassy, Ballsbridge
Posted on Monday, 31 August 2009

A chewy, cuboid-shaped, fruit-flavoured CAR

I was in the cinema with an ex-girlfriend and an ad for Bulmers Cider came on. My ex asked, 'Why do they have a different name for Bulmers in England and up North?'

At the time I wasn't really sure and I just replied, 'I suppose it's a bit like Opel down South and Vauxhall in the North.'

She stared at me blankly for a couple of seconds and responded, 'But I thought they were called Starburst here.'

Needless to say I erupted into laughter, not to the liking of those around me.

Overheard by Barry, Cineworld
Posted on Saturday, 22 August 2009

At least he was honest

Was drinking in Temple Bar and went outside for a smoke. I spotted two gardaí across the street collaring two teens.

Guard: 'In accordance with the law, I'm now going to search you for drugs. Before I start, do you have anything on you you shouldn't have?'

One teen replied: 'Yeah, me brother's shoes.'

Overheard by silverbullitt, Temple Bar
Posted on Thursday, 20 August 2009

The meaning of free

Bought a bag of frozen garlic mushrooms flashed with price €2.40 plus 30 per cent extra free. They scanned through at €5.20, I went to the customer services desk where the girl told me:

'Yes, €2.40 was the normal price, but as they have the 30 per cent extra free the price is €5.20.'

Overheard by Jenny, Tesco, Clare Hall
Posted on Wednesday, 19 August 2009

Guinness: purveyors of fine stews

My wife and I are American and visited Ireland last week. On the train from Galway back to Dublin we overheard four other tourists discussing food in Ireland.

Tourist Lady #1: 'Last night I tried some bangers and mash, it was pretty good.'

Tourist Lady #2: 'Yeah? You should try Guinness stew sometime,it's sooo good!'

Tourist Lady #1: 'Stew?! I thought Guinness only made beer?'

I wanted to slap her.

Overheard by Brent, train between Galway and Dublin
Posted on Tuesday, 18 August 2009

Very expensive pie

Was standing in a queue at Spar and a woman was in front of me buying an apple pie, this is how the conversation went:

'This is ridiculous, €13.08 for an apple pie, what sort of shop is this charging that much for an apple pie?'

Cashier: 'Er, that's the best before date.'

Cue sniggers of laughter from the rest of the queue, and the cashier trying not to laugh!!

Overheard by Sinners, Spar, by St Pat's Cathedral
Posted on Saturday, 15 August 2009

Schoolboy

Walking to work down Leinster Road, Rathmines one morning. The lollypop lady is letting a few kids cross the road, the traffic has all stopped. Just as the last kid has made it safely across a 30-something-year-old stubbly-suited fella does a tippity-toes run across while he can. A taxi driver shouts out:

'Well, you're a bleedin' hairy schoolboy, aren't ya?'

Overheard by Helen, Rathmines
Posted on Thursday, 13 August 2009

Winding up Ronan Keating

I was at one of the first showings of *I Keano* a few years ago in the Olympia, when I noticed that Ronan Keating was sitting a few rows in front of me. Just before the show started a group of shams, who were a few rows behind me also saw Ronan. Then they were trying to get his attention.

Lad: 'Ronan!'

No response from Ronan.

Lad: 'Ronan!!'

No response from Ronan again.

Lad (even louder): 'RONAN!!!!!!!'

Ronan turns around.

Lad: 'Sorry, bud, I thought you were someone else.'

Overheard by Anonymous, Olympia Theatre
Posted on Monday, 10 August 2009

Never work with kids

At the International Street Festival, guy doing his act pulls out this kid, about ten-years-old, to help with his act. He gets to the part where he's going to juggle fire and asks the kid, clearly taking the mick given the kid's age, if he has a lighter.

To which the kid replies, 'Naw, bud, left it at home.'

Overheard by Freckles, Merrion Square
Posted on Sunday, 9 August 2009

Should have said 'Big Boat'

One-year-old was asleep in the back seat so I opted to go on a Sunday morning drive around Northwall docks. I drove over to where there was a huge ferry. I said:

'Oh, look, there's the ferry.'

Our three-and-a-half-year-old asked: 'Where Dad? Is it a real fairy?'

Overheard by Anonymous, in the car, Northwall
Posted on Sunday, 9 August 2009

Giraffe in my bedroom

I was in our bedroom and my wife was in the hallway outside our three-year-old's room. My wife says, 'There's a draft coming out of Nessa's room.'

Me: 'Is it a big one?'

My wife: 'Yes, a big draft.'

Nessa came running over, looked into her room and said defiantly:

'There's no giraffe in here!'

Overheard by Anonymous, my house, Dublin
Posted on Saturday, 8 August 2009

Slinky girl

Going down the stairs in Stephen's Green, my friend and I heard this gem from the girls in front of us:

'Jaysus, I'm going to let gravity win, I feel like a feckin' slinky going down these yokes!'

Overheard by Sara, St Stephen's Green Shopping Centre
Posted on Friday, 7 August 2009

Mars bar messer

In the middle of an Irish test, one of the lads in the class is clearly struggling. He gets called by the teacher to the front of the class, the teacher hands him a euro and says,

'Get me a Mars bar out of the vending machine right outside the door there.'

The pupil walks off looking relieved. Twenty minutes go by and he still hasn't returned, then suddenly he walks in the door, looks at the teacher and says,

'Do you want an ordinary Mars bar or a Mars Delight?'

The whole class burst out laughing and the teacher angrily sent him back to his seat and took his euro back.

Overheard by Paul, the Kings hospital
Posted on Thursday, 6 August 2009

Full Metal Jacket

Working behind the bar one night a few weeks ago. Two guys at the counter having a discussion that is starting to get heated.

Fella #1: 'Don't start wih me, I've a machete and

chainsaw in me shed and a shotgun under me bed, you don't wanna see them!'

Fella #2 replies: 'Well, I've a f***in' tank in my attic, you don't hear me bragging.'

Everyone was rolling around laughing.

Overheard by Paddy, Stoneybatter

Posted on Wednesday, 5 August 2009

That time again

On the way into work early in the morning when the bus turns up with the driver all smiles and welcomes. A young girl goes up and throws a load of shrapnel into the machine thing to pay her fare. The driver goes,

'That time of the week, is it?'

To which the young one replies in a hearty attempt at banter,

'No, that time of the month!'

You could feel the cringing in the air!

Overheard by Conor, no. 70 bus

Posted on Friday, 31 July 2009

A standing ovulation, if you please

At the Celtic woman concert in Powerscourt, at the end the MC was asking for a final shot of the audience as it was a live recording. However, instead of asking for a standing ovation he asked for a standing ovulation!

Overheard by Sarah, Enniskerry
Posted on Thursday, 30 July 2009

Cheese please

I was at a deli counter when I overheard this American tourist in front of me placing his order:

'Oh hi, I'll have a bagel with eh ... um ... uh ... what kinda cheese do you have?'

The girl who was serving him looked him up and down as if he was a dope and says to him in her finest Dublin accent,

'Grrated or sliiiced.'

The look on his face was class. 'No Swiss then huh?'

Overheard by Gillian, at a deli counter in west Dublin
Posted on Monday, 27 July 2009

U2 fans outside Croker

Leaving Croke Park after the U2 gig. People were taking photos of Croke Park and the reflection of it in the Royal Canal, a lovely scene. A fella turns to his mate and says,

'Ah look, they must be mad U2 fans, taking pictures of Croker. They must think they'll never see Croke Park again.'

Then after a short pause: 'Or else they're from Leitrim'

Overheard by Barbara, after U2 gig
Posted on Saturday, 25 July 2009

Dyno-sore head

It's lunchtime on Dublin's Parnell Street. There are about ten or 12 people in Wacker's Pet Shop, mainly mothers with their kids who are on school holidays. And then there's this lanky twenty-something-year-old guy with a crooked stance and his forehead pressed up to a terrarium tank. He looks bewildered. Tapping on the glass of the tank, he mutters to himself:

'Jaysus, dat's de smallest bleedin' dyno-sore I've ever seeeen, man!'

Overheard by John H., Wacker's Pet Shop, Parnell Street
Posted on Wednesday, 22 July 2009

Multitalented cat

We got a new kitten and while watching him play on the floor with a piece of paper I said to my husband:

'We should get him a ball of wool.'

To which my daughter asks, 'Why, can cats knit?'

Overheard by Louie, sitting on my sofa
Posted on Tuesday, 21 July 2009

Still down with the kids

Two gardaí at Oxegen were walking past me as I was walking through the blue camp. One turns to a few girls nearby and asks, 'Who's on tomorrow girls?'

The girls respond with a few artists' names.

'Ooooooh Lady Gaga, we'll have to go see her tomorrow, Pat. I say she'd be savage.'

His colleague replies: 'Definitely! We'll go so. I love that one, "Poker Face", powerful tune.'

Nice to see they're interested in more than fighting crime!

Overheard by b24fan, Oxegen '09
Posted on Monday, 20 July 2009

A bit Irish!

One day recently I got fed up searching around the local Tesco for several of the items on my list – all favourites in our house and all well-known brands – so I handed the list to a staffer who carefully scrutinised it, then said:

'Ah no, missus, we've none of them, ever since the "Change for good" we only stock what the people want!'

Overheard by Anonymous, the local Tesco
Posted on Friday, 17 July 2009

Isn't that the whole idea?

On the no. 42 bus on the way into town.

Girl (to her friend): 'Did you ever notice when you put fake tan on ... everything is browner.'

Overheard by Anonymous, no. 42 bus
Posted on Tuesday, 14 July 2009

A mother's love

Passing by Centra in Maynooth, a little fella about five-years-old says to his Ma, 'Thanks Ma, I love this ice-cream.'

His Ma replied dead serious, 'You're welcome, ya little skitzo.'

Overheard by gizmo, Maynooth

Posted on Monday, 13 July 2009

Hey, whatever passes the day

After meeting a particularly attractive country girl, idle small talk lead us to discuss funny and bizarre events we had witnessed on public transport. She informed me that on one occasion she got on the no. 46a six stops from town, from which the driver asked her to remain standing beside him as he didn't know the way.

I responded: 'Are sure he wasn't just having a laugh?'

To which she sweetly and confidently replied: 'No, I even had to tell him where to pull over and even when to indicate.'

I wondered how many attempts the driver had before he found someone innocent enough?

Overheard by Amused, BBQ in South Dublin

Posted on Tuesday, 7 July 2009

Rod Stewart

Overheard at the Rod Stewart concert at the memorabilia stand.

'Jaysus! Rod is God but there is no f**king way he's getting 15 yoyos off me for a bleedin' mug.'

Overheard by Anonymous, Rod Stewart concert, RDS

Posted on Monday, 6 July 2009

Dublin Zoo line-up?

Visiting Dublin Zoo on Saturday. Was standing looking at one of the animals and a little girl beside me pipes up:

'Oh mammy, look he is coming over to us.'

The mother replies: 'Don't worry darling, he can't see you, it's one-way glass!'

Overheard by Trish, Dublin Zoo
Posted on Thursday, 2 July 2009

Dressing up

In the hairdresser's at Hallowe'en, hairdresser says to woman in chair next to me:

'Is ur young fella dressin' up this evenin'?'

To which woman replies: 'Yes, he's dressing up as Lucifer.'

Hairdresser stops, thinks, chews gum a bit harder and eventually says:

'Is tha' ur man in Cinderella?'

Overheard by Deirdre, hairdresser's in Ongar, Clonsilla
Posted on Tuesday, 30 June 2009

How hygienic

Standing in the kitchen at a party in a friend's house talking to one of the lads. Another lad comes over and starts washing his hands in the sink with washing-up liquid.

I say: 'Why are you washing your hands with washing-up liquid?'

The guy beside me immediately goes: 'Because he's a mug.'

Overheard by Jess, party in Rathgar
Posted on Sunday, 28 June 2009

Invisible rope

More seen not heard.

Six young lads about seven or eight years-old, sitting on either side of the road leading in to our estate and pulling a rope across the road. I slowed the car to a crawl so I wouldn't get caught by the rope only to discover it was an invisible rope! Looked in my rear mirror as I drove on to discover the lads cracking up laughing at me.

Overheard by Neado, Baldoyle
Posted on Monday, 29 June 2009

Terrier on the train

A lady was taking her Yorkshire Terrier on the train. The dog seemed very agitated on the journey and wouldn't keep still, constantly whimpering and barking. From another seat, I heard in a big Northern Ireland accent:

'Hey missus, your dog's not train trained.'

The carriage was in stitches.

Overheard by J, Dublin–Belfast train
Posted on Sunday, 28 June 2009

Ok, then...

We had an end of year Irish test the other day and our teacher was correcting them. He calls on my friend Brian.

'Brian, did you copy off the boy beside you?'

'No, sir,' he replies.

'Ok, then,' says the teacher. 'First line: Is mise Tom.'

We were in stitches.

Overheard by usher, a classroom, south Dublin
Posted on Thursday, 25 June 2009

Smoking strictly prohibited

I was strolling down O'Connell Street on my lunch break when I got held up by a passing Luas. On my left were two gardaí talking to some zonked smoke hound. Garda #1 turns to his partner and says,

'Can you believe this fella?'

Garda #2 just raises his eyes to heaven. Garda #1 gives the smoke hound a school master's scowl and says,

'Do you think it's acceptable to be smoking heroin on one of Dublin's main thoroughfares?'

To which the smoke hound replies,

'But what do ya mean? I was smoking in the phone box.'

Overheard by Ronnie, O'Connell Street
Posted on Wednesday, 24 June 2009

Moore Street exercise programme

Two women on Moore Street discussing their husbands' health. One woman's husband had just had a heart bypass operation and was told he needed to start some gentle exercise, the other retorted by saying,

'The only exercise my Jimmy gets is jumping to bleedin' conclusions.'

Overheard by Adrian, Moore Street
Posted on Tuesday, 23 June 2009

Colour blind

Walking down Henry Street a while back, I overheard a man explaining his understanding of what colour blindness is to his elderly mother. He said:

'Colour blindness is when you can't see colours right, you see everything in black and white.'

Overheard by Billy, Henry Street
Posted on Monday, 22 June 2009

Luas crash

On the red line Luas when it hits a bus near Busáras. Loud crash, glass door bursts in, tram lurches and grinds to a halt. A moment of silence.

'What was that?' said an aul' wan.

'Well, it's not a feckin' puncture,' says the hubby.

Aul' wan sniffs in disdain and looks out the window.

Overheard by Stephen, Luas
Posted on Friday, 19 June 2009

Starbucks have everything except for ...

In Starbucks. I decide to order a caramel frappuccino.

Your one, serving me (in monotone): 'Sorry we have no coffee left.'

Overheard by Anonymous, Starbucks, Liffey Valley
Posted on Thursday, 18 June 2009

Comma-cal

Junior Cert. 2009, English Paper 1.

Examiner: 'Okay, we just have a correction in the exam.'

(Everybody expecting something major.)

Examiner: 'Okay, page 5, paragraph 6, 10 lines down and 5 words in ... insert a comma.'

Overheard by Joey, Lucan
Posted on Thursday, 18 June 2009

Future WAGs

Walking through Penneys and two girls (velour tracksuits, high pony-tails, the works) are shopping.

Blonde girl: 'I'd love dat dress, but me legs will look huge in it.'

(Bear in mind she was about a size 8.)

Brunette: 'All ye need is a birre confidence, Amy.

You don't want to be payin' for yer own drinks all yer life, do ye?'

Overheard by Jessi, Penneys, Omni Shopping Centre, Santry
Posted on Thursday, 18 June 2009

Take that!

At the Take That concert in Croke Park. The queue outside the ladies' during an interval was very long. Not wanting to miss the show a few carefree ladies decided to avail of the under-used gents' facility, but were surprised to be met by a guy in his thirties complaining.

'What the f**k are ye women doing in here in the gents toilets?'

Most were quietly embarrassed, but were delighted to hear a young Dublin lady respond, 'What the f**k are you doing at a Take That concert?' before watching the guy squirm back out the toilet door with no more to say for himself.

Overheard by Anonymous, Croke Park
Posted on Monday, 15 June 2009

Don't try this at home

Was at the street artist festival and a juggler was juggling knives. When he was finished he says,

'Remember, kids, don't do this at home, go to a friend's house.'

Overheard by Conor Warren, Merrion Square
Posted on Sunday, 14 June 2009

What a way to greet a friend!

Was in Heatons when I overheard this greeting from two women!

Lady #1: 'Hey how are you?'

Lady #2: 'Fancy meeting you f**kin out here out in this f**king shopping centre, in this f**king shop!!'

Overheard by Louise, Charlestown Finglas Shopping Centre
Posted on Friday, 12 June 2009

Plan B

While playing to a packed house in the New Theatre Temple Bar, Dublin singer/songwriter Keith Burke forgot the words in the middle of one of his songs. Within seconds a voice called out,

'Sing one ye know!'

Overheard by Peter, New Theatre Temple Bar
Posted on Wednesday, 10 June 2009

Fowl play

Out having a few beers with some American lads that were over from California to work with us for a few weeks. One of the Yanks calls over a young barmaid to buy a round.

Yank: 'Can I have five pints of Guinness, two pints of Bulmers and I'll have a Wild Turkey?'

Barmaid, looking slightly puzzled, walks away and comes back ten minutes later, with Guinness and cider and says,

'Sorry we've no turkey, but I can get you a chicken sandwich.'

Overheard by Wally, Laurels Pub, Clondalkin
Posted on Wednesday, 10 June 2009

Great aunt

Sitting on the Luas, a woman in her early thirties comes on screaming down the mobile phone.

'I don't effing care how long you're with her, you're only 19 for eff sake and that young wan is what ... 16? But that's not even what's really p*ssing me off, you've made me a great-aunt at the ripe old age of 32, ya little b**tard.'

Overheard by Sarah, Jervis stop
Posted on Tuesday, 9 June 2009

Shake your time

While standing in a lengthy queue of men in the cinema toilets, which were all full as the movie we had just watched had ended, someone in the queue ahead grew impatient with one of the men using a urinal and shouts:

'You shake it on your own time!'

Overheard by John, queue for toilet in the cinema
on Parnell Street
Posted on Saturday, 6 June 2009

An oe exhibit

One afternoon in the National Museum, at an exhibition of 5,000 year-old bodies that had been found preserved in Irish bogs. After viewing one of these bodies, an elderly Dublin woman turned to her son and said with heart-felt sympathy:

'Ah, the lord 'ave mercy on 'im, I bet he never thought he was goin' to end up in here.'

Overheard by Deirdre, National Museum, Dublin
Posted on Friday, 5 June 2009

High school

Studying Engineering, I was in one of our advanced Maths classes. The elderly Maths lecturer had just filled several blackboards full of maths equations (the type that require use of half the alphabet) on several blackboards all along the front of the lecture theatre.

On nearing the end of space the blackboards had to offer, he suddenly realised he had made a mistake in his calculations, he stopped writing and looked back at the boards of chalk, and said:

'I think I dropped an e.'

The whole lecture theatre erupted and he had no idea why.

Overheard by Hugh, at a lecture in Trinity College Dublin
Posted on Tuesday, 2 June 2009

Taxi mam

At an 18-year-old's birthday celebrations. We had gone to a mate's house after the pub for a few more drinks and we were all pretty locked. As the mate's house was miles out of our way the birthday girl decides to call a taxi to get home, in her drunken state she accidentally rings her parents' house:

Birthday girl: 'Hello, can we get a taxi, please?'

Her Mum: 'Mary, is that you?'

Birthday girl: 'Yeah, whose dah? How do ya know me name?'

Her Mum: 'Mary, this is your mam.'

Birthday girl (still thinking she had called the rank): 'What are you doin' there, Ma??'

Overheard by Anonymous, outskirts of the city
Posted on Tuesday, 26 May 2009

Peace envoy

While walking past one of Dublin's unsavoury bars, I overheard three tough lads arguing.
While two of these were ready to go head-to-head, the third, in all his wisdom, tried to defuse the situation and said to his pal,

'Don't hit 'em wit ur fists Tomo, hit em with ur wurds.'

I immediately thought this guy should join the UN.

Overheard by Damien, Dublin city centre
Posted on Tuesday, 26 May 2009

Denier?

Guy and girl, both mid-twenties, in a cafe in NUI Maynooth.

Guy: 'Saw a great documentary on the Holocaust last night.'

Girl: 'Hmmm ...'

Guy: 'Do you even know what the Holocaust was?'

Girl: 'Wasn't it the nuclear thing?'

Overheard by Robert, cafe in NUI Maynooth
Posted on Tuesday, 26 May 2009

Empties!

A lounge girl, new on the job and a bit nervous, clearing glasses from a table full of old guys. As she is being handed an empty glass from one of the guys, he says,

'Another deadman.'

Lounge girl: 'Another deadman, I'll get it for you now.'

Overheard by Catherine, pub in Ballinteer
Posted on Monday, 25 May 2009

Monday blues

First thing in the morning, double science Junior Cert. revision of Biology and human reproduction.

Teacher: 'What happens to make babies, people?'

Class look to desk.

Teacher: 'Ok, ok, what is the first thing we need?'

A student down the back: 'Alcohol!'

Class and teacher crack up.

Overheard by Ginge, school
Posted on Tuesday, 19 May 2009

Recession hits Dublin

Seen not heard.

You know it is a recession when you see your neighbour washing his own Merc.

Observed by Tommy
Posted on Friday, 15 May 2009

Taste the value

Was in Dunnes when I seen a lady and her 20-something daughter shopping.

Daughter: 'Ma, look at these trifles!'

Ma: 'Nah, got them last week and they are disgusting, no taste off them at all.'

Daughter: 'But they're half price.'

Ma: 'Well, give us two there so.'

Overheard by Traykool, Dunnes, Tallaght
Posted on Friday, 15 May 2009

Recession is grinding jobs to a halt

Middle-aged Dub on the bus into town.

'Yeh, me daughter's hours have been changed now. She's startin' at different times each day, dey've stagnated dem.'

Overheard by Royal Commuter, on the bus
Posted on Wednesday, 13 May 2009

Dublin population explosion

I was on the DART from town yesterday and two young chaps, wearing tracksuits with the bottoms tucked into their socks, were discussing the current population of the country when one spouted:

'Sure, there's more people living in Dublin than there is in the whole of Ireland.'

Overheard by Suzanne, on the DART
Posted on Wednesday, 13 May 2009

Recession car sale

Girl with a 'For Sale' sign on her Toyota Celica walks into the chipper.

Italian fella taking the orders says: 'What do ya want for the car?'

Her reply: 'A battered sausage and chips, please.'

Think he was waiting for the keys till she realised what he said!!

Overheard by Lisa, Raheny chipper
Posted on Saturday, 9 May 2009

Chivalry isn't dead

Myself and a big gang of friends were on the Nitelink home one night a few years ago. Most of the lads were fairly poleaxed but having great craic.

Next thing, three girls get on the bus and sit down right in the middle of us all. One of the lads starts chancing his arm with the loudest and best-looking one of the three. The other girls weren't talking at all.

Just as we're about to get off the bus, one of the lads, who was completely hammered and hadn't opened his mouth, turns to the quiet girl sitting across from him and goes:

'Here, you wouldn't just ... sort us out ... would you?'

Overheard by Colonel Montoya, no. 51 Nitelink
Posted on Thursday, 7 May 2009

How to empty a Luas

On the Luas coming out of town one afternoon during the week. As we got to Blackhorse the driver made an announcement:

'Ladies and gents, there are two plain clothes ticket inspectors getting on at this stop, so could you please have your tickets at hand for convenience. Thank you.'

When we pulled up to the stop two people did get on and about 50 got off and stood on the platform, clearly waiting on the next Luas.

When we pulled away the driver got back on the intercom, laughing and said:

'I was only joking, there's no such thing as a plain clothes ticket inspector, I just wanted to see how many people got on without paying!!'

Overheard by Lynn, on the Luas
Posted on Wednesday, 6 May 2009

And I didn't even intend it ...

Down my local on Saturday, this guy introduced me to the woman he was talking to and said:

'This is Toona and she's from Norway'.

I said 'Aha' and he chuckled and said:

'Good one, Frank.' (For younger readers, A-ha were a 1980s band from Norway.)

Overheard by Frank, Donoghue's Kilmainham
Posted on Wednesday, 6 May 2009

The ratio of red versus blue in Croke Park

In the toilets before the match, I overheard two guys discussing the ratio of red to blue fans in the crowd.

'No, I'd say it's about 70/40.'

Overheard by Dave, at the Munster vs Leinster
semi-final in Croke Park
Posted on Tuesday, 5 May 2009

Multitasking

More seen than heard.

Was on the bus at Terenure Cross and the bus was trying to turn right when a car came in front of it. The driver of the car stopped and waved the bus to go on ahead. So he gave the driver a thumbs-up and the middle finger. At the same time.

Overheard by Sarah, no. 15 bus at Terenure Cross
Posted on Saturday, 2 May 2009

Recession bites

Aul' fella chatting to his younger workmate.

Aul' fella: 'Do you be going out drinking much these days?'(Referring to the recession, etc.)

Workmate: 'Nah, not much mate, can't afford it.'

Aul' fella: 'Jaysus, I'm the same, I used to drink seven nights a week, now I only drink five nights! And I love me gargle now.'

Overheard by Liam, a certain college in Dublin
Posted on Thursday, 30 April 2009

Health versus finance (start at an early age)

I was walking through Trinity College beside the big rugby pitch. I see two teenage boys skating along the pathway when one of them falls off his skateboard and hits the ground. The other one gets off his skateboard and comes running to him asking,

'Jaysus, are you alright?'

To which the other one replies,

'I'm fine but I think I hurt me hand.'

'Oh God, you're bleeding, let's buy you some tissues and clean it up.'

'I am not paying for a packet of tissues! I'll go get some free from McDonalds.'

Overheard by JASEM, Trinity College Dublin
Posted on Sunday, 26 April 2009

Hot wheels

On the train from Dublin to the midlands. Ticket collector leans out the window of the carriage and starts to talk on his mobile to the driver.

'Hello Jim, you're producing a lot of smoke up there, I think you are on fire.'

Not sure what happened next but it's a good thing the passengers all knew about this!

Overheard by C, on a train leaving Dublin
Posted on Sunday, 26 April 2009

Bank raid?

My boyfriend phoned his bank to make an enquiry, the bank manager answered the phone

and sounded a little flustered. He asked my boyfriend to hold the line as all the assistants were 'tied up' for the moment.

Overheard by Anonymous, Bank of Ireland
Posted on Tuesday, 22 April 2008

Restaurant warehouse

One night my boyfriend and I decided to grab some dinner in TGI Friday's as he had never been before.

The waitress hands him the menu booklet and with wide eyes he exclaims to the whole restaurant.

'Size a this! Like a bleedin' Argos catalogue!'

Overheard by Emma, TGI Friday's, Blackrock
Posted on Monday, 20 April 2009

Computer whizz

Two girls discussing their friends ineptitude at using computers:

'I mean she's, like, completely computer un-literate.'

Overheard by Marty, Aungier Street
Posted on Monday, 20 April 2009

Malehyde

Sitting at the kitchen table with my dad when my sister comes home. She sits down and starts complaining that she has spent the whole day doing a piece for her Leaving Cert. Art project.

'We sat there all day sculpting these bodies from the Bog of Allen. They're preserved by some chemical.'

My dad interrupts: 'Formaldehyde?'

Sister replies with a confused look: 'No! From the midlands!'

Overheard by Samantha, Horse's Mouth
Posted on Tuesday, 14 April 2009

A mammy's best friend

In the canteen in work last week, all the mammies were talking about their daughters. One of them starts talking about her own daughter and how she gets on her nerves. Then she says without a hint of irony:

'Oh, but I love me dog though, she's an aul' pet.'

Overheard by Alan, work canteen
Posted on Tuesday, 14 April 2009

Typical Dublin date

I was going out with a young Dublin lad last year in college, he wasn't the romantic type so I was quite surprised when he rang.

Patrick: 'Hey, I'm taking you out for dinner! Meet me outside Trinity Front Arch in 15 minutes.'

So I went and he was there with his friend.

Me (to the friend): 'Oh! Are you coming for dinner too?'

Patrick: 'Yeah, well he can get us into Trinity Art Society social evening, free food and wine for all.'

Apt treatment from a Dublin lad!!

Overheard by Claire, Trinity Front Arch
Posted on Sunday, 12 April 2009

Magic carpet

Seen a Middle Eastern looking guy banging a small carpet on the wall of a balcony on the second floor of a flat in Ballymun when some local guy shouts up:

'What's wrong, will it not start?'

Overheard by Phil, Ballymun
Posted on Thursday, 9 April 2009

Triple decker

On the no. 39 coming from town late on Paddy's night. The bus was jam-packed. Some fella went to get off on the Navan Road and says to the bus driver,

'Just so you know, there are people standing

upstairs and sitting on the staircase, I barely got down in time.'

To which the bus driver replied real sarky,

'Well, what do ya want me to tell them? Sit on the roof?'

And he just drove off.

Overheard by luceylou, no. 39 bus
Posted on Sunday, 29 March 2009

Looking at it philosophically

Slightly upset young female colleague reflects ruefully:

'I'm not getting on too well with me Mam these days. But then, the two of us do go back a long way.'

Overheard by Patricius, Monday morning chat in the office
Posted on Saturday, 28 March 2009

He won't be using that one again!

Standing having a smoke outside a Dublin nightclub early one night. Overheard the following between a guy and girl.

Guy: 'Six-foot penguin.'

Girl: 'Wha?'

Guy: 'Jus tot a six-foot penguin would break the ice.'

Girl: 'Five-foot two-inch woman.'

Guy: 'I don't get it.'

Girl: 'If ya don't f**k off a five-foot two-inch woman will break your face!'

Overheard by Jen, Heaven Nightclub
Posted on Saturday, 28 March 2009

Heavy music

On the no. 123 bus and two girls were sitting in front of me. Both of them had their iPods and were comparing playlists or whatever. The blonde one asks to flick through her friend's music. Then with a look of genuine surprise she turns around and says,

'Oh my God, your iPod feels heavier than mine. Is that because you've more music on it?'

Overheard by Sean, no. 123 bus
Posted on Friday, 27 March 2009

Neither a borrower nor a lender be

Two suits were walking in front of me out of Pearse Street DART Station the other day when one of them says,

'If I had a cent for every time I had to listen to people moaning about this bloody recession, I'd be rich.'

The other lad then asks, 'Would you loan me a score then?'

To which the first lad replies, 'Ya see, it's requests like that is what has us in this situation in the first place.'

The response to that was, 'Tight b**tard.'

Overheard by Maho, Pearse Street DART Station
Posted on Thursday, 26 March 2009

Mammy's boy!

Waiting at passport control in Dublin Airport, there was a group of lads coming home from a weekend away.

Lad #1 (joking): 'Hurry up, I can't wait to get home and see me ma!'

Lad #2: 'I can't wait to get home to see your ma either!'

Put a smile on everyone's face in the queue.

Overheard by Anonymous, Dublin Airport
Posted on Wednesday, 25 March 2009

Holy eyes!

My auntie had just come back from the optician after having an eye test and announced that she had 'stigmata' in her eye (she had astigmatism!).

Overheard by Nikki, on the phone
Posted on Wednesday, 25 March 2009

Paddy the pick-pocketer

A few months ago I was standing at the Luas stop at Stephen's Green when an announcement was made over the PA.

'Ladies and gentlemen, we would like to inform you that there are pick-pocketers working in the area, so please mind your belongings.'

This was followed by:

'Paddy Murphy I can see ya and if ya don't go home I'll tell yer ma ya wer at it again!'

Overheard by Anonymous, Luas stop Stephen's Green
Posted on Tuesday, 24 March 2009

Probably waiting years to use that

Was standing waiting to pay on the no. 84 bus and a little old lady in front of me asked the driver the following question:

'Does this bus stop near the Shanganah Cemetery?'

To which the driver instantly replied:

'Sure, what would you be doing going there, love? You're not dead yet!'

Overheard by Peter, no.84 bus on Eden Quay
Posted on Tuesday, 24 March 2009

The Multipurpose spoon

In the Spar on DCU campus, a group of Dublin teenagers in front of me in the queue.

Boy #1: 'Have yiz ever seen those half-spoon half-fork yokes?'

Boy #2: 'Yeah, der called sporks!'

Boy #1: 'But have yiz ever seen one with a knife on de handel too?'

Boy #2: 'Jaysus, is it a f**kin' Swiss Army Spork?!'

Overheard by Anonymous, Spar, DCU
Posted on Sunday, 22 March 2009

I'm not askin', I'm tellin'

A student of mine works at a café in the city centre. He was about to serve a woman who had a three-year-old boy with her.

'D'ya wanna cookie?' asked the woman looking down at her kid.

'I wanna jelly snake,' came the response.

'D'ya wanna cookie?'

'No, I wanna jelly snake.'

'D'ya wanna cookie?'

'No, I want a jelly snake!'

'What part of "D'ya wanna cookie?" don't you understand?'

Screwing up his face and pointing at the jelly snakes in desperation.

'I want ... (sob) ... a jelly ... (sniff) ... snake ... (sob, sniff).'

'So you want a jelly snake,' says my student.

'Ye,' says the woman.

Overheard by Jamie, Dublin School, Merrion Square
Posted on Wednesday, 18 March 2009

Dublin wit

Having arrived home from England on a short break with two South African friends, we asked a car park attendant at the airport which was the quickest way to the Naas dual carriageway.

'Get a f**king helicopter,' came the reply as he went away about his business.

Overheard by Timmy, Dublin Airport
Posted on Wednesday, 18 March 2009

My parade

Standing on College Green, getting squashed as the St Patrick's Day Parade makes its way down the road. A D4-type woman squeezes in near me, obviously looking for a good viewing spot, then shouts back to her other half:

'It's no good, all I can see are those f**king leprechaun hats and cameras.'

Summed up the day for me.

Overheard by Sindy, St Patrick's Day Parade
Posted on Wednesday, 17 March 2009

Lovelorn

Heartbroken lad of about 15 on the bus with his mates and having a drunken rant.

'She doesn't even know his name, he's saved in her phone as "Starbucks Guy".'

Overheard by ac Slater, no. 49 bus
Posted on Monday, 16 March 2009

Couldn't put it better themselves!

'I'll never listen to a politician again. Everything they ever say is just unremitigating dribble!'

Overheard by Patricius, tea room at work
Posted on Monday, 16 March 2009

Christmas card

Overheard a teenage girl and her dad in Eason's book shop discussing what they had bought for Christmas presents.

Girl: 'Did you get mum her card?'

Dad: 'Oh, I knew I forgot something. I wonder where I left it?'

Girl: 'What do you mean where you left it?'

Dad: 'I've given her the same card for the last 16 years.'

Girl: 'She hasn't copped on?'

Dad: 'Well, I never dated it.'

Overheard by Cíara, Eason, O'Connell Street
Posted on Monday, 16 March 2009

Plane crazy

Standing behind an elderly Dublin woman at the till in the newsagent's, I heard her ask the check-out girl:

'Howya love, d'ya have any of them ticket yokes for the airport?'

After a few seconds of looking a bit confused, the girl twigs it and says, 'For the toll?'

And she goes 'Yeah'.

Obviously doesn't hit the Northside too often.

Overheard by Gizmo, newsagent's in Tallaght
Posted on Sunday, 15 March 2009

The big tree

A girl in her teens from down the country was due to meet people after a GAA match outside The Big Tree pub near Croker. She was getting a little upset on her mobile phone and cried:

'You said you'd meet me outside the big tree, but there's loads of bloody big trees around here!'

Overheard by Keith, near Croke Park
Posted on Monday, 16 March 2009

Mind your own business

Last week I had to visit my local doctor's surgery in Knocklyon. While I was waiting to see the doctor a pregnant woman came into the room

and sat down next to a middle-aged man.
Nobody was talking, so I guess the middle-aged
man decided to break the silence. He turned to
the pregnant woman and asked:

'What do you hope it is?'

With that she replied: 'My husband's.'

Overheard by Anonymous, doctor's surgery
Posted on Friday, 13 March 2009

The helpful Dub

I was driving down Dorset Street. There was a
man in a wheelchair crossing the road at some
road works. The lights turned green and he was
still in the middle of the road, the first car was a
taxi driven by a foreign national man who
started having a go at the man in the wheelchair.

One of Dublin's finest, in a tracksuit and hoodie,
shouts at the taxi driver:

'Hey fuggie, leave the cripple alone,' and
continued on his way happy to help.

Wrong on so many levels.

Overheard by Carl, Dorset Street
Posted on Thursday, 12 March 2009

Flat tyre

A friend's wife rang him in some distress, her car
had a flat tyre. He asked her did she think she'd
be able to change it. She replied that maybe it'd
be ok to drive as it was only flat at the bottom.

Overheard by Ben, Dublin city centre
Posted on Wednesday, 11 March 2009

American tile

I was due to meet up with a few English cousins of mine in the well known Dublin bar The Mercantile. After half an hour waiting, I gave them a call only to find out that they were driving around the city with some confused taxi man looking for the American Tile.

Overheard by Ben, Dublin city centre
Posted on Wednesday, 11 March 2009

Lost in translation

Years ago when a friend started working in a local supermarket, elderly people would come into the shop and hand him a list of their shopping, which he would collect for them. On one occasion an elderly lady asked for one litre of milk and 40 More (meaning the cigarette brand More). She was a little shocked when a few minutes later he showed up with a trolley full of 41 litres of milk.

Overheard by Ben, Tallaght
Posted on Wednesday, 11 March 2009

Is it a DART? Is it a plane?

On the DART into town the other day, sitting near two head-de-balls, who were debating the merits of the DART over the bus. One wonders aloud if there were toilets in the space between the two carriages when the other, getting all high and mighty, shouts at him:

'Don't be bleedin' stupid, dat's where the pilot sits, ya tic!'

Overheard by Dave, on the DART
Posted on Sunday, 8 March 2009

Wheelchair parking

Was in the car with my friend when she went to park in a disabled spot. I told her she couldn't park there as it was a wheelchair spot, to which she replied:

'Well, I've never seen a wheelchair park in one.'

Overheard by Jen, in car
Posted on Saturday, 7 March 2009

Pyjamas backlash begins

More overseen than overheard.

In a café in Finglas, a sign in the window simply states:

'Appropriate dress must be worn at all times, NO PYJAMAS!'

Overheard by Lozz, Finglas Village
Posted on Tuesday, 3 March 2009

How many recessions were there?!

While travelling on the no. 27 bus from Coolock to town, sitting in front of me was a young, well-dressed man and a very elderly lady. The man was talking on the phone with a worried voice, and after he had hung up the phone the lady leaned over to him and asked:

'Is this your first recession, love? Awh, well, God love ye!'

Overheard by Casey, no. 27 bus from Coolock to town
Posted on Tuesday, 3 March 2009

Dilemmas, dilemmas

On the DART one afternoon, sitting beside a woman with two very small boys who were eating lollipops. The youngest hands his back to the mother and says,

'Nuff, Mam.'

The woman hands it to the other boy and says,

'Here, you can finish your brother's.'

The brother, now holding a lollipop in each hand, gazes from one to the other and says wistfully,

'Do you know what Mam?'

'What's that?'

'I wish I had two tongues!'

Overheard by Bob, on the DART
Posted on Friday, 27 February 2009

Send bill to ...

While checking payment forms at work today for a certain toll payment company in Dublin.

One field on the form asks for 'Name on credit card'. One genius entered 'MasterCard'.

Overheard by Anonymous, at work
Posted on Friday, 27 February 2009

Stupid is as stupid does

At work today, after a day of blunders and mishaps, my co-worker had had enough.

'Why do things that happen to stupid people keep happening to me?' she gasped out of frustration.

Overheard by Dan, Microsoft
Posted on Friday, 27 February 2009

On your bike love!

Walking through Temple Bar a few months ago. Overheard a very loud conversation between three howyas deciding where to go. One of the girls shouts out to her mate:

'We'll go in 'ere, der's loadsa goodlookin' fellas in here.'

On cue, a garda on his bike cycles by:

'Go away out of that, the tide wouldn't take you out love.'

Everyone within ten metres burst into laughter.

Overheard by Iano, Temple Bar
Posted on Thursday, 26 February 2009

Little tarts

At mass, the priest is reading some announcements from the parish newsletter.

Priest: 'Cake sale across the road today in aid of St Vincent de Paul. Perhaps you might want to take home a little tart for yourself?'

Cue sniggers and snorts from the few who were listening.

Overheard by Jim, Santry
Posted on Thursday, 26 February 2009

Deli-cious

In a Spar getting a roll and a guy was in front of me at the deli.

He meant to ask the lady for a box of potato cubes, but what came out with was 'can I have a box of cutato pubes?'

Overheard by Shani, in Spar
Posted on Wednesday, 18 February 2009

My friend, the car hunter

The other day, our swimming team was doing some bag-packing in Kilnamanagh Shopping Centre to raise funds. As we were leaving, my dad tells us to watch out for cars when we were walking across the car park.

My friend (who is car mad) says: 'Ooh, look, a Jaguar GT!'

Overheard by Oisín, Kilnamanagh Shopping Centre
Posted on Sunday, 15 February 2009

The best scare tactic

On the bus, group of guys aged 17–18 were discussing their younger sisters. One of them tells the others what he'd say to a guy his sister brings home:

'Just remember, anything you do to her, I'll do to you.'

Overheard by JenTheSmurf, no. 46a bus
Posted on Sunday, 15 February 2009

Dumb Dub on dort

One typical D4-style girl says to her friend,

'I don't see why they have doors on both sides.'

Overheard by Kevin, DART
Posted on Saturday, 14 February 2009

A memory like an elephant

It was our Junior Cert. a couple of years ago and we were all sitting around in the examination centre waiting for the examiner to get there. When she finally arrived we realised we knew the woman – a rather large woman at that – she had been a substitute for us the year earlier.

As she put her things down, she looked up to see one of the messers of the class and, in a condescending tone, said,

'Oh, I remember you.'

And of course being on his top form, he belts out,

'Oh yeah? Well elephants never forget!'

Needless to say he was ejected from the exam.

Overheard by E.N., examination centre, school
Posted on Saturday, 7 February 2009

Super Kate Mosse

I overheard two D4-heads in Waterstone's Bookstore. One girl picks up *Sepulchre* by Kate Mosse.

Girl #1: 'Ooh, this is Kate Moss's new book!'

Girl #2: 'She's a supermodel and a writer too? Wow, that girl is so talented!'

Overheard by Eileen, Waterstone's,
Jervis Street Shopping Centre
Posted on Thursday, 5 February 2009

Next Luas

I was on the Luas at Smithfield heading out of Dublin at 6.00 p.m. and it was pretty full as usual. People were trying to push on when the driver said:

'There's no point in trying to get on, there is another one right behind. The driver is Tom

Cruise and the ticket inspector is Pamela
Anderson!'

Overheard by Nigel, Luas
Posted on Thursday, 5 February 2009

Got a light?

Taking a short-cut through Sheriff Street to get
to Connolly Station, I spotted two unmarked
Garda cars and one squad car parked in the
middle of the road outside a terrace of houses.

As I got closer, six people left the terraced
house, all wearing rubber gloves and carrying
CSI-type briefcases with 'Drug Squad' written on
their jackets. I couldn't see anyone arrested or
any contraband been taken away. None the less,
very impressive.

By the time I reached the house, the three Garda
cars had sped off. As I walked past the house, a
door opened two houses down and out walked
a pale-looking young man who could barely

open his eyes (it was during daylight hours) with a massive joint in his mouth. He turned to me and asked:

'You gotta light?'

Overheard by Joe, Sheriff Street

Posted on Monday, 2 February 2009

Sci-Fi Junior Cert.

Working in Eason's Liffey Valley the other day when a woman comes up and asks me for a 'Sharp Science Fiction Calculator, for me son doin' his Junior Cert.'

Overheard by Steve H., Eason, Liffey Valley

Posted on Friday, 30 January 2009

Bitchy

I attended a gay black-tie event over the summer and part of the night was that a limo would pick you up from one venue and bring you to the next. We were sharing the limo with four strangers. One of the girls remarks on another who was wearing a revealing cocktail dress:

'Jaysus would ya look at yer wan trying to be Paris Hilton.'

To which her flamboyant male friend replied:

'More like Paris Travelodge, ya mean!'

Overheard by Stevie, limo on George's Street, Dublin

Posted on Sunday, 25 January 2009

Overly interested teacher!

Was in school the other day and it was one of those mornings where the temperature was below zero. As the whole class was sitting on the side with the radiator, the German teacher asked one student to move to the other side of the class. Here's how the discussion went.

Teacher: 'Come on, move over to the other side it's not that cold.'

Student: 'But, miss, it's freezing.'

Teacher: 'Don't worry, I'll harden you up fairly quick.'

Student (quick as a flash): 'Sorry, miss, you're not my type!'

We were in stitches!

Overheard by Benno, boring German class
Posted on Sunday, 25 January 2009

Recruitment recession-style

I was at the gym this morning when I overheard two old guys talking. One old guy says to the other old guy:

'These young people today don't know what a recession is at all. I remember the last recession. When a fella died they used to advertise in the paper where the fella worked.'

Overheard by Stephen, gym
Posted on Friday, 23 January 2009

You're (not) hired

I was interviewing for part-time staff in my store and asked one girl:

'What is the most valuable thing you can bring to the company?'

To which she replied: 'Eh ... probably my watch.'

Overheard by Kim, in my store on Grafton Street
Posted on Wednesday, 21 January 2009

Air rage

This summer on an Aer Lingus flight into Dublin there was some bother with the front door. We were all sitting on the plane getting really annoyed and after about ten minutes the pilot comes on the speaker and says:

'Sorry about that ladies and gentlemen, just a bit of bother getting the steps to the front of the plane due to Ryanair leaving their crap everywhere.'

Overheard by Aine, Aer Lingus flight
Posted on Saturday, 17 January 2009

Need a bigger car

Was helping my brother to wash his car (a small old Micra) outside our house. It was all soaped up and brushed, but I had no hose to wash soap off and was using a watering can. A van slows down, window rolls down and driver says to me.

'Jaysus, love, you're wasting your time, it'll never bleedin' grow!'

Overheard by Susie, outside my house in Dundrum
Posted on Friday, 16 January 2009

Recession hits everyone!

I was on O'Connell Street in Dublin a few weeks back and two young lads about 15-years-old were walking towards me. They were wearing tracksuits and looked like real Dubs.

They had just come out of McDonald's and one of the lads holding up his caramel ice-cream sundae says to his mate:

'Jaysus, Maccers have gone real stingey on the sauce in their ice-creams.'

To which his mate replied: 'Ah, that's the f**kin' recession for ya man!'

Kind teacher

Teacher in Home Economics class points at information for one particular lad to take down off the board.

Teacher: 'This is for you.'

Pupil: 'Ah, thanks, miss, I always wanted a white board!'

Cinderella

Overheard while watching a performance of *Cinderella* at a theatre in the city centre which will remain anonymous. Almost all of the jokes in the show were either toilet humour or smutty. We had just got to the bit where the evil Abanaza was trying to persuade the Dame to hand over the magic lamp in exchange for a new one.

Abanaza: 'Is there anything old and dirty I can exchange?'

Disgruntled parent: 'There is your script for a start.'

No room at de Inn

A teacher acquaintance told me that the rehearsals for her nativity play with her Senior Infants went just fine. However on the night of the performance ...

Joseph and a heavily pregnant six-year-old Mary were looking for accommodation.

The first inn (knock-knock): 'Is there any room?'

Reply: 'The inn is full, there is no room.'

The second inn (knock-knock): 'Is there any room?'

Reply: 'The inn is full, there is no room.'

The third inn (knock-knock): 'Is there any room?'

Reply: 'The inn is full, there is no room. Fuck off!'

Entire audience in stitches.

Overheard by Eoin, from my teacher friend
Posted on Friday, 9 January 2009

Pig ignorant

The brother, at the end of a queue at the meat counter in Dunnes the weekend of the pig meat crisis.

Lady to butcher: 'You're not listenin'! I don't want pork products – I want twelve slices of ham!'

Overheard by Eoin, Dunnes Stores
Posted on Friday, 9 January 2009

Dangerous young wans!

My sister was on her way to the Olympia theatre to meet me and my mam to see a panto. She walked past this drunk aul' fella and the aul' fella said:

'Do yi know, yous bleedin' young wans are so gorgeous yur bleedin' dangerous.'

Overheard by Liam-o, on way to Olympia theatre

Posted on Friday, 9 January 2009

What's the difference?

I was getting potato chunks at the hot food counter in Dunnes Stores. When the lady filled the chunks into a paper cup some of them looked burnt. I asked her if she could take out the burnt ones.

'They're not burnt,' she said, 'they are just brown because they were in the oven too long.'

Overheard by Anonymous, Pavilion Swords

Posted on Tuesday, 6 January 2009

Dublin Zoo no. 2

On a recent visit to Dublin Zoo, a crowd of about 20 people had gathered at the gorilla enclosure. The mother gorilla proceeded to have a 'number two', which she skilfully caught and proceeded to eat (fresh)! This she repeated a couple of times and it was finished off by the baby gorilla helping itself to the leftovers stuck to her rear end.

There was much howling and squealing from the gathered crowd. One guy turned to his wife and said:

'And you think I'm disgusting!'

Overheard by Mo, Dublin Zoo
Posted on Tuesday, 6 January 2009

Could have sworn it was jalapeno peppers?

Work for a pizza company, could tell you any amount of stories. Funniest by far though, a lad rings up and asks for 'Al Pacino' peppers on his pizza. Didn't have the heart to tell him....

Overheard by Foxy, Pizza place, Clondalkin
Posted on Monday, 5 January 2009

Astronomically challenged

After three weeks of leaden skies, the cloud finally breaks at about 8 p.m. one evening in September 2008.

D4 girl #1: 'Wow, doesn't the moon look bright!'

D4 girl #2: 'Emm ... that's the sun!'

Well, it had been a very overcast summer.

Overheard by Patricius, Top deck of no. 46A approaching
Dún Laoghaire Station
Posted on Friday, 2 January 2009

Seven sacraments

Teacher: 'What are the seven sacraments?'

Student: 'Yer baptism, yer confirmation, yer debs, yer stag night!'

Overheard by Mary, can't tell but it is a Dublin school
Posted on Tuesday, 23 December 2008

The best days of your life?

In Leaving Cert. Art class some years ago, it was my week to be the subject that the class drew. After some time one of the lads shouts very loudly:

'Miss, how do you draw a double chin?'

Overheard by Traykool, in school some years ago
Posted on Monday, 22 December 2008

Murder in Trinity

Walking through Trinity with a friend, I pointed to the 1937 Reading Room and said:

'*Michael Collins* was shot in there.'

My friend in reply: 'I thought he was shot in Cork.'

Overheard by Mark, Trinity
Posted on Saturday, 20 December 2008

The fruit trade

I was passing a stall on Moore Street run by two women – I'd say a mother and daughter.

A foreign lady (possibly Italian) looks confusedly at a sign saying 'Wine Apples' on the stall and asks what it means.

One of the women says, 'Pomegranates luv.'

The Italian then asks, 'What do you do with it?'

The traders look at each other in disbelief and the daughter roars back, 'Ya eat it!'

Overheard by Mark, Moore Street
Posted on Saturday, 20 December 2008

First date

Misfortunate foreign girl with very little English on a date, listening to a non-stop babbling idiot who (loudly and patronisingly slowly) declares:

'Did you know that only 1 per cent of communication is verbal?!'

Overheard by Maria, Beer Garden
Posted on Wednesday, 17 December 2008

Some are feeling the pinch more than others

Doing some Christmas shopping in Boots and overheard a group of girls talking about the state of the economy.

'She wha'? Returning a book of stamps?'

'A jaysus, dis repression is bleedin' mental!'

Overheard by Anonymous, Boots Blanchardstown
Posted on Tuesday, 16 December 2008

Enlightenment with chips and curry sauce

My local Chinese takeaway has a large pot-bellied Buddha statue sitting on the counter. I was waiting for my order when in walked three lads. First in was a bald, roly-poly chap who turned to his friends and said:

'See, I told you I'm a preferred customer here ... they've even got a statue of me on the counter.'

Overheard by Kev, the Fortune Cookie in Woodstown

Posted on Tuesday, 16 December 2008

What's cheap is dear!

The girlfriend's mother decided to join this economising lark when she bought a box of two dozen lovely little Christmas cards at the 'right price'. She wrote most of them, then sent them in the post. Only when she got back home did she read the message on the last couple, it said:

'Just a little card to say – a little gift is on its way!'

Overheard by Anonymous, Artane

Posted on Sunday, 14 December 2008

Fruit of the forest yoga

My mother-in-law says she really knows how to look after her pet parrot. She feeds him 'fruit and nuts and yoga'!

Overheard by Thomas, mother-in-law's

Posted on Saturday, 13 December 2008

Famous spire?

I was meeting an English friend in town as he was over for a weekend.

Me: 'Meet me on O'Connell Street by the Spire, I'll be there in a few.'

To which he replies: 'What the hell is the Spire and where is O'Connell Street?'

Me: 'Well, where are ya and I'll come find you.'

Him: 'I'm on the main Dublin Street, the one with that big needle thing on it.'

Overheard by Jen, O'Connell Street
Posted on Friday, 12 December 2008

Scalded mickey

Working at a roadside on underground telecom cables. A stunning young lady jogs past.

Workmate shouts: 'Take it easy, luv, ye'll boil yer waters.'

Without missing a stride she replies: 'Ye needn't worry, ye'll never scald yer mickey in them.'

Overheard by Tommy, Crumlin
Posted on Friday, 12 December 2008

Northside olympics

A few years ago, in the run up to the Special Olympics in Ireland, I was holding a collection in the office for the 'Support an Athlete' programme.

Now, I'm a proper Northside Dub and have the accent to go with it, and I work with this Southside babe from Foxrock. Lovely, but a bit dim.

I walked up to her desk and told her that I was fundraising for 'Support an Athlete'. She smiled her lovely smile and said: 'That's wonderful.'

But then with a puzzled look asked: 'Who's Natalie?'

Overheard by Kev, at work
Posted on Thursday, 11 December 2008

Philosophical

I caught the end of what must have been a riveting conversation between two blokes sitting in a Dublin bar.

Bloke #1: 'They only make a limited number of those ya know.'

Bloke #2: 'They only make a limited number of everything.'

Bloke #1: 'True, true.'

Overheard by Jake, Dublin bar across from Jervis Centre
Posted on Wednesday, 10 December 2008

See through

Overheard in Blackrock Shopping Centre.

Girl #1: 'I didn't know you could see through aluminium.'

Girl #2: 'Ya can't ya muppet.'

Girl #1: 'Ya f**kin' can.'

Girl #2: 'Ya f**kin' can't.'

Girl #1: 'Did ya never hear of aluminium windows?'

Overheard by Anonymous, Blackrock
Posted on Wednesday, 10 December 2008

J. K. Rowling perhaps?

A woman talking on her mobile: 'So, are you going to the Quidditch match tonight then?'

Overheard by Sorcha, crossing a road in Dublin
Posted on Friday, 5 December 2008

Do some research first!

At the Helix to see the RTE Concert Orchestra playing the music overlay to the classic film *The Wizard of Oz*. At the interval a mother and child push their way onto the seat beside us. On the mobile the mother is shouting:

'We're leavin', we're going to Granda's. It's crap, it's not a show. It's a film, a film with a manky band in front!'

Overheard by batman, Helix, DCU
Posted on Thursday, 4 December 2008

Handmade

Was in Superquinn and there was one of those stalls giving out free pizza samples. A man goes up and tastes some.

Man: 'Ah, dat's not too bad, how much is it?'

Posh lady replies: '€7.99'

Man: 'Wha?! That's bleedin expensive!'

Posh lady replies: 'Well, they are handmade.'

Man: 'Well, of course they're handmade, they're hardly gonna make 'em with their feckin' toes!'

Overheard by Adam, Superquinn, Blackrock
Posted on Wednesday, 3 December 2008

Idiots at the cinema

Went to see *I Am Legend* in the cinema and all through the trailers and for the intro of the film these little s**ts of about 15 were all laughing and taking the piss. Then the title comes up on the screen and one goes:

'I am Leg End? What the f**k?'

Everyone in the cinema starts laughing and someone shouts back '*I Am Legend*, ya thick!'

They were quiet for the rest of the film.

Overheard by Anonymous, UCI
Posted on Tuesday, 2 December 2008

Is it me you're looking for?

Working in a CD shop you often get odd questions and people singing at you, but one day a really frustrating woman came in. After about 15 minutes of questions she asks her final and best.

'Oh have you got that song? I can't remember who sings it, or what it's called, it goes like ...'

(About to start singing but stops.) 'Oh, actually, I wouldn't inflict my singing on you! Do you know it?'

My co-worker looks at her calmly and says, 'Oh yea, it's "Hello", Lionel Richie.'

The woman looks thoughtful and says, 'Oh is it?'

My co-worker just sighs. I had to leave the counter I was laughing that much.

Overheard by Frustrated, work, CD store
Posted on Tuesday, 2 December 2008

Christmas would be great if it wasn't for that Jesus chap ...

In the reception of a public sector agency, two staff chatting about Christmas and its associated meanings:

'I like Christianity, but I'm not too keen on the religious side.'

Overheard by Anonymous, reception of a government agency
Posted on Tuesday, 2 December 2008

Enda O'Donnell!

At *Top Gear Live* in the RDS last weekend, the Fine Gael leader Enda Kenny was shaking hands with one of the show-goers and his teenage daughter. As Enda walks off to enjoy the exhibition, the man says to his daughter, 'Do you not know who that is?'

The daughter replies that she 'hasn't a clue' and her father tells her in all seriousness, 'It's Daniel O'Donnell's older brother!'

Overheard by David, Top Gear Live, RDS

Posted on Monday, 1 December 2008

Ask a stupid question

I was on the DART on my way into town when a young group of lads sat opposite me. One of them looked out the window, noticed the HSS out at sea and decided to ask a rather odd question.

Lad #1: 'Do you think you'd get arrested for sailing underneath the HSS?'

Lad #2 shook his head: 'No.'

Lad #1: 'Why not?'

Lad #2 sighed at his friend's stupidity: 'Because they can't arrest a corpse.'

Overheard by Fry, on the DART

Posted on Tuesday, 25 November 2008

Monkee business

I was at the bar waiting to get served when an aul' fella noticed a young fella standing next to me wearing an Elvis T-shirt.

Aul' fella: 'Here, young fella, can I ask ye a question? What's with the T-shirt? I mean, you're far too young to remember Elvis.'

Young fella: 'I grew up listening to all the classics, Elvis, The Beatles, The Beach Boys, The Monkees ...'

Aul' fella: 'Jaysis! The Monkees?! Well, if ye come back here wearin' a Monkee's T-shirt then you're a bleedin' daydream believer!'

To which the young fella wittily replied: 'Oh, I'm a believer!'

Overheard by Fry, Madigan's Pub on O'Connell Street
Posted on Tuesday, 25 November 2008

Questions of academic interest

Our lecturer – the embodiment of the distinguished professor stereotype, older man, grey hair, glasses, beard, etc. – was giving us instructions on how to carry out our studies/experiments for our final year projects.

Professor: 'Now, you need to ask yourselves these questions – "Who, what, where, when, why? (pause) Kind of like the morning after the night before – Who'd you do it with, what did you do, where did you ...?" '

Overheard by Smileyface, lecture hall, Trinity
Posted on Sunday, 23 November 2008

I'm a cat...

On Hallowe'en at around 11 p.m. we got a knock on the door.

I thought it was a bit late for trick or treaters, but lo and behold there was a girl of about 15 standing there.

She was wearing a cut-off belly top that used to be an Adidas jacket, a belt around her waist and Ugg boots on. She was texting on her phone and didn't even look up when she said 'trick or tree'.

I, not wanting to give the remaining sweets to someone who put in no effort whatsoever, inquired what she was supposed to be?

And with that she turned around revealing one leg of a pair of giraffe print tights stuffed with tissue.

She sighed and said: 'Oi'm a bleedin' cah!'

Overheard by Anonymous, my front door
Posted on Saturday, 22 November 2008

That is my cheese!

At the cinema a few weeks ago queuing for popcorn. Fella in front of me was after ordering nachos and cheese. When the girl working behind the counter handed it to him, he asked her what kind of cheese it was.

To which she replied: 'That's nacho cheese.'

'It is,' he replied highly indignant, 'I just paid for it.'

Overheard by Amused in cinema, Dublin

Posted on Friday, 21 November 2008

The rare 'nuttin' animal

I'm an Austrian who's been here now for a few years, so I am starting to get *overheardindublin.com*. But initially when I arrived I obviously didn't.

I went to the zoo after having been here for a month. When standing at the African plains, next to me a child and her mother had a little conversation going.

Child (pointing with her finger): 'Ma, what kinda animal is dat?'

Mother (in strong Dublin accent): 'Nuttin.'

Me, turning head around wildly to spot this animal called 'nuttin' which I've never heard of or seen.

Overheard by Anonymous, Dublin Zoo

Posted on Thursday, 20 November 2008

Just like on the telly

Was doing work experience in a solicitor's firm. One day to get me out of the office they sent me down to the District Court with a trainee. I'm sitting there in the court room with a vague idea about what's going on, when out of nowhere the woman beside me turns round to me with serious face and goes.

'Jaysus, it's awfully like *Judge Judy*, isn't it?'

I had to bite the inside of my mouth to stop myself from laughing.

Overheard by Anonymous, District Court
Posted on Thursday, 20 November 2008

An eye opener

Waiting in an optician's last week for a friend of mine, when an old boy in front of me stares down at a magazine on the seat and says:

'What's the shagging point of leaving magazines around, if we could read them we wouldn't be here in the first place!'

Overheard by Derek, local optician's
Posted on Thursday, 20 November 2008

The 'urban fox'

My friend Cathy's mother was visiting her from the US. On the first evening in Cathy's house (which is near a main road) they heard sounds outside. Mother asked what it was, to which Cathy replies, 'Oh, it's just an urban fox.' Conversation moves on.

Next day the mother is occupying herself sightseeing alone and is on a bus when she notices the squealing of the brakes sounds just like the noise she heard the night before. She (randomly) puts two and two together and assumes that the 'urban fox' is some sort of informal name for the transport system!

Cathy arrives home from work that evening and asks her mother what she got up to on her first day in Dublin.

Mother (smiling blissfully): 'Oh it was

wonderful! But I'm absolutely exhausted now – I was riding the urban fox all day.'

Overheard by Marie, college friend
Posted on Wednesday, 19 November 2008

Role reversal

An Indian man was powering up Dame Street and passed an older Dublin man (flat cap and all) who was walking in the same direction. The Dublin man, who clearly knew the Indian man, hit him on the back of the head with his morning Metro, shocking the young Indian man, and said:

'We must all look the same to you, do we!?'

Shock, recognition and finally jovial chat ensued as they walked on together.

Overheard by Anonymous, Dame Street
Posted on Wednesday, 19 November 2008

... and that concludes today's work ethic lesson

Office temp to office employee: 'Is it ok if I sit at your desk during your lunch hour? I can answer your phone for you?'

Office employee: 'Work away, but don't bother with the calls, I never answer it anyway. It'll stop eventually.'

Overheard by Al, at work in Dublin
Posted on Tuesday, 18 November 2008

Don't like that film

Sitting in the apartment a few nights ago with my girlfriend and asked her if she wanted to watch a film on TV.

She asks: 'What's it about?'

I looked it up and told her it was about a psychopathic killer.

She says: 'Is there nothing better on? I don't want to watch a film about a psychic caterpillar.'

Overheard by Dave, at my apartment in Dublin city centre
Posted on Tuesday, 18 November 2008

Child at breaking point

Was walking through Dunnes Stores with my three-year-old daughter last week and you could see the child was bored shopping with me. Suddenly she stopped in the middle of the store and said:

'Oh my god will you just buy something before I have a nervous breakdown!'

Everyone started laughing at her, which got her more annoyed, and she stormed out of the shop with me trailing after her.

Overheard by missy, Dunnes, Blanchardstown
Posted on Monday, 17 November 2008

That would have been a rather unpleasant way to go ...

A few weeks back I took a short-cut to the DART Station by jumping over a wall and startled an elderly man who was walking his dog.

Elderly man: 'Jaysus! Ye nearly made me sh*t me heart outta me arse!'

Overheard by Fry, Baldoyle
Posted on Monday, 17 November 2008

Dirty driver

Overseen rather than overheard.

Good few years ago driving behind a van covered in dust, someone had written on the back in the dirt.

'If you think this van is dirty, try spending a night with the driver.'

Overheard by Anonymous, N11
Posted on Sunday, 16 November 2008

Back o' da bus

I was on my way home on the no. 32A after work, stuck in traffic during rush hour, sitting up top. Two school kids were sitting at the very back looking out the window and noticed that a person we had passed a while back had now caught up with the bus.

Kid #1: 'Feckin' hell that guy's caught up with us already, he must be a fast walker!'

To which kid #2 replied: 'You never know, he could just be a slow runner.'

Overheard by Fry, on the no. 32A
Posted on Sunday, 16 November 2008

... and then she got her P45

After a particularly bumpy landing in Dublin, our friendly crew announced:

'Please remain in your seats with your seatbelts fastened while the captain taxis what's left of our airplane to the gate!'

Overheard by Anonymous, Aer Lingus flight from Heathrow
Posted on Friday, 14 November 2008

Ah, to be a kid again ...

So I'm doing a jigsaw of a map of Europe with my four-year-old niece.

Niece: 'What does that say?'

Me: 'That says "English Channel" '

Niece: 'What does that mean?'

Me: 'That's the name of that particular bit of sea.'

Her mother/my sister: 'You know, some people swim across that!'

Niece: 'How do they get across the letters?'

Overheard by Dave, my sister's house
Posted on Friday, 14 November 2008

Boxed in!

In a manual handling and lifting class, we were practising how to lift boxes the proper way. As you can guess, it was a bit unnerving doing this in front of everybody. It's this guy's turn when he pipes up in a true Dub accent and says:

'Jaysus! I've never been so scared of a measly empty box in me darn life!'

Well, that broke the tension.

Overheard by Tobi, IWA, Clontarf
Posted on Friday, 14 November 2008

Ladies please

A young lad on a bus was tapped on the shoulder by an elderly lady pointing to a pregnant woman standing by his seat and said: 'If you were half a man you'd give that lady your seat.'

He said: 'Missus, if I was half a man I'd be in a bleedin' circus!'

Overheard by Barry, no. 46a bus heading out of town
Posted on Thursday, 13 November 2008

It's in the bag

Standing at the bus stop and there was a Dub guy in front of me, baseball cap, the works and carrying a hold-all. Guy passing by sees him and says, 'Howya Jim, how's it goin'?' Jim says 'OK', and mate asks him what's he got in the holdall.

Jim: 'Drills'

Mate: 'How many?'

Jim: 'Guess'

Mate: 'If I guess right will you give us one?'

Jim: 'If you guess right I'll give you both.'

Mate: 'Ok ... eh, three?'

Overheard by jmac, no. 78a bus stop on way to town
Posted on Thursday, 13 November 2008

Just plain nuts ...

A bloke I work with told me this story.

When he worked as a barman there was the usual bunch of aul' fellas who regularly drank in

his pub. One day one of them asked him for a bag of nuts. He asked the aul' fella what kind of nuts he wanted and the aul' fella asked what kinds there were. The barman listed off a variety, salted, dry roasted, honey roasted and pistachios. The aul' fella asked him what pistachios were like as he'd never had them. He decides to buy a bag and promptly opens it and pours a few pistachios into his mouth. He chews and crunches his way through a few more before saying:

'Give us a bag of ordinary ones, these are very hard.'

Overheard by Mr Spling, pub in Dalkey
Posted on Thursday, 13 November 2008

She really didn't belong in the pit!

As the first support act for Kanye West started their third song (it was two djs and one rapper), I heard a girl in the row behind me go, 'Jesus, Kanye's great, isn't he?'

Overheard by Anonymous, the pit, Kanye West concert
Posted on Monday, 10 November 2008

The price of jeans!

Got text from my daughter shopping on Thomas Street.

'Hi, just down on Thomas St looking at veg. Give you a laugh ..."two over-jeans for €1.50".'

Thicko here in central France couldn't understand so texted back to say that.

She texted back, 'Mum, what rhymes with over-jeans?'

Still thick so she rang, 'AUBERGINES!'

Overheard by Jane, from daughter down on Thomas Street
Posted on Saturday, 8 November 2008

Living on different planets?

Was sitting on the top deck of the no. 46a and two young lads in front of me, one of them reading the paper, turns around to his friend and says:

'Jaysus look at this. Mother of nine to be sentenced tomorrow for shoplifting.'

His mate turned to him and said: 'Bleedin' hell ... that's very young to be a mother!'

Overheard by saoirse66, on no. 46a on way to town
Posted on Wednesday, 5 November 2008

Credit crunch get-out clause

A man walks into the bank and asks can he change his mortgage to interest-only repayments, as he is out of work. The girl replies and informs him that he has to be earning at least €120k to change to interest-only.

To that the man replies: 'Why the feck would I be looking for interest-only if I was earning €120k? Use your fecking head!'

Overheard by N, TSB Bank
Posted on Monday, 3 November 2008

Fare dodgers

On the Luas a while ago when the tram broke down. The driver came on the speakers saying, 'Sorry folks, we'll just be delayed for a few minutes.'

Two young Dub lads, about ten-year-old started complaining extremely loudly, saying, 'Jaysus, this is ridiculous, I have to be in school, crappy Luas.'

Then after a few minutes of their moaning one of them shouts, 'Glad I didn't buy a bleedin' ticket.'

Overheard by Caoimhe, on the Luas
Posted on Sunday, 2 November 2008

At Tescos

I was stacking shelves near the fruit and veg section of Tesco. This woman came over and asked in a really strong Dublin accent, 'Have you got any man-get-out?'

I had no idea what she was talking about so I just said that we hadn't. I only realised about six hours later that she was talking about mangetout!

Overheard by Aoife, working in Tesco
Posted on Sunday, 2 November 2008

Not a fan of walking

(Three lovely girls down the back of the bus, playing Rihanna loud enough so that everyone can enjoy it.)

Girl #1: 'Ah here, Tammie this bus is taking bleedin' ages, d'ya wanna gerroff an walk?'

Girl #2: 'What do I look like, a bleedin' treadmill?'

Overheard by Anonymous, the no. 7 bus
Posted on Saturday, 1 November 2008

She's had her chips

Was in a chipper in Stillorgan recently. Girl in queue in front of me ordered two singles.

Guy behind counter: 'Do you want them wrapped separate or together?'

Girl: 'Eh, would you wrap one of them separate, please?'

Overheard by denman, takeaway in Stillorgan
Posted on Thursday, 30 October 2008

The spiral!

No. 16a on a Saturday is always full of tourists coming from the airport. Woman on bus starts conversation with American couple by asking 'have you been in Dublin long?' You could see conversation could only go downhill seeing as they were sitting on a bus coming from the airport with their suitcases on their knees.

When bus gets to O'Connell Street she points out the window and says,

'See that, that's our famous landmark, once you know where that is you can't get lost in Dublin. Just ask anyone to show you where the spiral is and you won't get lost.'

And as they are getting off the bus she is shouting, 'Don't forget, once you can see the spiral you won't get lost.'

Overheard by Trish, no. 16A coming from airport
Posted on Thursday, 30 October 2008

Straight to the point

Seen rather than heard.

At the recent student fees protest, one fellow

had a sign saying 'AC/DC for Slane'. Another one had a sign saying 'fees are bollix'.

Overheard by Caroline, streets of Dublin
Posted on Thursday, 30 October 2008

Foot-patrol

Waiting to start work on Eden Quay in Dublin (yes, I'm a bus driver) when one of the usual wasters that can be found on the boardwalk on a sunny day is approached by two gardaí. They search him for drugs, they ask him, 'Have you anything in your shoes?'

To which he replies, 'Me feet.'

Overheard by M, Eden Quay
Posted on Wednesday, 29 October 2008

Irish welcome

Was at an Ireland vs South Africa rugby game about two years ago. One guy in the crowd was giving Bryan Habana awful abuse (nothing racist, shouting out the usual 'Habana you're sh*te!' kinda stuff). This was going on for the whole game and he had us all in stitches.

With Ireland up by a good few points, Habana then got injured. A voice over the tannoy then said: 'Bryan Habana retires to be replaced by ...'

To which the guy shouts out: 'Retired? Ah Jaysus, Habana you're not that bad!'

Overheard by Jack, Lansdowne Road
Posted on Tuesday, 28 October 2008

Who's in control

My niece's first time at the cinema this weekend. While waiting for the film to start she was getting impatient, she demanded to know very loudly,

'Could whoever has the remote control please press start!'

Overheard by Anonymous, cinema
Posted on Sunday, 26 October 2008

Ideal future career

Teaching in a sixth class in an all-boys school, I was asking the pupils what they would like to be when they were older. I was getting the usual responses: carpenter, doctor, electrician, etc. until one lad, without batting an eyelid said:

'I want to be a stay-at-home mom, they do nothing!'

I couldn't contain the laughter, and nor could the class!

Overheard by Obbie, primary school, Wicklow
Posted on Saturday, 25 October 2008

Batteries for babies!

My two nieces arrived with their two children, one a three-year-old and the other a newborn baby. When the newborn started crying the three-year-old turned and asked:

'Where do her batteries go?'

Overheard by Marie, at home
Posted on Thursday, 23 October 2008

Foot-in-mouth

A few years ago, in the Phoenix Park watching the marathon runners go by. We were about 20 yards from the top of the run, which then went downhill towards the park gate. My husband took to shouting encouragement at any laggers, but we had to quickly drag him away after he shouted at one struggling woman:

'Keep going ma'm! You're nearly over the hill!'

Overheard by Anonymous, near the Furry Glen, Phoenix Park
Posted on Thursday, 23 October 2008

Emergency smoke

Coming home on the last bus from Bray to Greystones on a dark wintry night. A man standing at a spot which is not a recognised bus stop stretches out his hand to stop the bus. Surprisingly enough the driver pulls in to pick up the passenger. I suppose he felt sorry for the man standing there in the drizzle with an unlit cigarette in one hand, swaying a bit. But instead of getting on the bus he gestures unsteadily with the cigarette and says, 'Got a light?'

The driver goes 'Ah for f**k's sake!' and drives off.

Overheard by Paul, on the bus from Bray to Greystones
Posted on Wednesday, 22 October 2008

The ideal gift

Two mid-twenties lads in the Omni Park Shopping Centre.

Lad #1: 'I have to get something for me dad's birthday, but what do you get for the 59-year-old that has everything?'

Lad #2: 'A time machine.'

Overheard by Dave, Omni Park, Santry
Posted on Wednesday, 22 October 2008

Many miles from home

Guy waking up on Nitelink: 'Are we in Firhouse yet?'

Me: 'No, we're in Blanch Village.'

Cue panic attack.

Overheard by Turlough, no. 39N
Posted on Wednesday, 22 October 2008

Car wash

Went to visit a mate working at a car wash. After a half hour or so a pretty badly dented VW Golf pulled in.

'A Wash 'n' Wax, please!'

'Do ya want me to iron it as well?!'

Overheard by Anonymous, car wash
Posted on Monday, 20 October 2008

Pandemonium in Croker

Was in Croke Park for Dublin v Tyrone. Before the match a man came over the intercom.

'In the event of an emergency you will hear this sound.'

Before they could play the sound, a guy behind me screams 'AAAAAAAAA!!!!!'

Overheard by Mastermind, Upper Cusack Stand, Dublin v Tyrone
Posted on Saturday, 18 October 2008

Well able for it

I had started college and one of the lads in the class came in trying to be the funny man and thought he'd wreck the teacher's head, so he said: 'Miss, I can't take down any notes, I'm dying of sexual exhaustion.'

He was fairly shocked when she said: 'Well you can try writing with your other hand so.'

Overheard by Rory, back of Economics class
Posted on Saturday, 18 October 2008

Taking the piss

Two aul' lads, both fond of a drink. One says to the other:

'Go on, fill this sample cup for me, I've a doctor's appointment later an' I've been on the rip for a week, he'll go through me.'

Other lad says no bother, takes the cup and does the needful.

Later that week, down the local, in comes the first lad, throws a packet of pills to the other: 'You've got a kidney infection.'

Overheard by Ray, local
Posted on Friday, 17 October 2008

Wave

I was out during a rare hot summer's day on Donabate beach. On the rocks with my six-year-old trying to find crabs when I heard a group of lads abuse a girl in the water.

'A tsunami wouldn't give you a wave.'

Overheard by paddy, Donabate beach
Posted on Friday, 17 October 2008

Praying out loud

In mass on Sunday we were all saying our individual prayers after communion. There was a boy (about three or four) saying his prayers out loudly.

'Please God will you look after mammy, daddy and all the people who were eaten by the angry giant in giant-land.'

Overheard by Les, Bray
Posted on Thursday, 16 October 2008

Wally's just not trying anymore

My daughter was looking at a *Where's Wally* book she'd just brought home from the library.

After a couple of pages she shouts: 'Ah mam! Someone has put a circle around Wally on all the pages!'

Overheard by Valerie, at home in Baldoyle
Posted on Wednesday, 15 October 2008

Painter's blues

Working on a building site, the painter was painting the walls of an office. Some wide cabinets were in each office and were about 9-inches from the wall. I asked him to make sure he painted the walls behind these too, and he said: 'What do you think I am? A bleedin' ventriloquist?'

Overheard by denman, building site in Dublin
Posted on Tuesday, 14 October 2008

Stating the obvious

'... mostly cloudy with scattered showers and the roads will be dry unless it's raining.'

Overheard by Dhollandia, weather report on Newstalk radio
Posted on Tuesday, 14 October 2008

Speed merchant

Myself and a friend were walking into the ILAC shopping centre on Henry Street. There was a middle-aged couple from the area walking in front of us. The woman was ahead of the man and walking at quite a fast pace when the man shouted out to her from behind.

'It's not a bleedin' motorbike I have under me arse, it's a pair of legs!'

Overheard by Ally, walking into the ILAC centre
Posted on Tuesday, 14 October 2008

One for the road

Outside our local pub a while back there was a commotion over who was going to drive the car home. One woman was asking her friends for help getting the keys off her husband. She shouts over to her friend:

'Mary will ya help me, he's not driving home in

108

that state. The last time he drove home like that, he hit everything but the bleedin' lotto.'

Overheard by Derek, local pub
Posted on Monday, 13 October 2008

Always get the girl's number!

On the bus home at around two in the morning, a young guy chatting up two girls.

Guy (to one of the girls): 'I'm good with numbers, but I'm really bad with names. If your name was a number, or had a digit in it, I'd remember it.'

Overheard by Smileyface, no. 7 Nitelink
Posted on Sunday, 12 October 2008

Mexican Scarface

My friend Thomas was cooking Mexican food and went to a shop in the city in search of sour cream. The interaction with the two shop girls went as follows.

Thomas: 'Excuse me, do you sell sour cream?'

Girl #1: 'Do we sell wha'?'

Thomas: 'Sour cream.'

Girl #2: 'Ya mean cream that's gone off like?'

Thomas: 'No. Sour cream for Mexican food.'

Girl #1: 'Eh. No. Never heard o' that.'

Thomas: 'Ok. Thanks.'

As Thomas leaves the shop he hears Girl #1 say to Girl #2:

'Sour cream! Who does your man think he is? F**kin Al Pacino or sumthin?!'

Overheard by Darragh, from my mate while
looking for sour cream
Posted on Wednesday, 8 October 2008

Double identity

In a chipper, a woman saying to a friend:

'We used to have a cat called Ben and when it gave birth it was called Ben Hur.'

Overheard by twobucktwo, a chipper in Bray
Posted on Wednesday, 8 October 2008

Religious worship D4-style

Posh Dublin lady to her friend: 'Oh my God, the new Manolo Blahnik section is open in BT's!'

Posh Friend: 'Really?'

Posh Lady: 'Seriously, it's like a shrine. I nearly genuflected on the way in.'

Overheard by Catherine, a gym in Dublin city centre
Posted on Tuesday, 7 October 2008

Stupid signs

Driving from Donegal to Oxegen a few years back with my friends. We pass a sign for 'Hidden Dips' when my friend Denise asks: 'Why are they putting the dips in the road if they are hiding them?'

Myself and my other friend just looked at each other and shook our heads.

Overheard by Linda, on route to Oxegen
Posted on Monday, 6 October 2008

A real Dub

Talking to old guy in pub. He asks me, 'Are you a Dub?' I said, 'Yeah, but my parents are culchies so I am not a proper Dub.'

The aul' guy says, 'Ah, but you're Irish, you're one of us and sure didn't your parents do the business in Dublin ... they are as good as Dubs.'

Overheard by Anonymous, pub with cheap drink
Posted on Monday, 6 October 2008

Drunken Saturday

I was sitting at a bus stop in Rathfarnham one Saturday morning when a drunk came over and started looking at the timetable. After a while he turned to me saying, 'Here you, what day is it?' so I told him it was Saturday.

He looked at the timetable for about ten seconds before turning to me again, 'Is it Saturday all day?'

Overheard by Eoghan, bus stop, Rathfarnham
Posted on Saturday, 4 October 2008

Culinary genius

During dinner at a work do recently, two colleagues were sitting side by side as the soup was dished up when the following conversation occurred.

Colleague #1: 'Pass the salt.'

Colleague #2 passes the salt and asks: 'Would you not like to taste it first?'

Colleague #1: 'No, why would I sure it's f**kin' white, isn't it?'

Colleague #2: 'I meant the soup, you muppet.'

Overheard by Anonymous, at a recent work do
Posted on Friday, 3 October 2008

Nice comeback

All-Ireland football final, Tyrone had beaten
Kerry. Tyrone supporter to Kerry supporter: 'The
Kingdom are f**ked, feck off back to the
Kingdom.'

The Kerry supporter smiles and says: 'Ah well, at
least when I get home I won't be looking at a
picture of the Queen on my money.'

Overheard by Anonymous, Croke Park
Posted on Thursday, 2 October 2008

What about the other 10 per cent?

Shortly before landing on a Ryanair flight to
Dublin the intercom goes through all the usual
and says at the end:

'Ninety per cent of all Ryanair flights have
landed ... '

My sister looks nervously at me, 'What happens
to the other 10 per cent?'

Overheard by el arto, on a Ryanair flight to Dublin
Posted on Wednesday, 1 October 2008

A dying dog's last days

A mate of mine had an old dog that was on his
last legs and it was decided to get him put down
for humane reasons. When his mam asked him
when he was going to bring Rusty to the vet for
the termination he replied that he planned to do
it on Monday.

The mother replied with a classic:

'Ah, would ya not wait until Thursday? There's

loads of dog food there and it would be a shame to see it go to waste!'

Overheard by Prendy, Tallaght
Posted on Tuesday, 30 September 2008

Psychic tour guide

On holiday a couple of years ago with my ma and da in America at Christmas time, which as everyone knows, the Americans refer to as 'the holidays'. We went for a tour of the original Coca Cola factory and at the end of the tour the guide says to us 'happy holidays'.

To which my dad says: 'How the f**k does she know we are on holidays?'

Overheard by Phil, on holiday in Atlanta, Georgia
Posted on Tuesday, 30 September 2008

What a headcase ...

Passing a group of drunks on the quays this morning at 10.30 a.m. One rather scruffy looking man, can in hand, approaches me.

'Redhead!' I continue past him. 'Redhead!' he calls me again and I look back quickly.

'Redheads are lovely heads.'

Brightened up my morning!

Overheard by Flopsy, Aston Quay

Posted on Monday, 29 September 2008

I'm not racist but ...

Standing in a long queue for a train ticket, black lady at the front with two or three kids, she was taking some time as she didn't seem to know where she was going. Two blokes behind me and one says to the other.

'Ah, bloody black people, always holding up the queue wherever I go, always one of them in the bank or a shop and they never seem to know what they want. I hate this, I normally check to see if there's one at the front of a queue. Jesus how long does it take to buy a bloody ticket?'

His mate agreed and then asked him what he was doing for the weekend, to which the first bloke replied:

'Oh, I'm going to the Festival of Cultures in Dún Laoghaire, we go every year, it's really great.'

Overheard by Brian, Connolly Station

Posted on Monday, 29 September 2008

You try!

I was out having a meal one night with my two sisters and we ordered a bottle of wine, the waiter was standing beside the table corking the bottle and he said to my sister 'you try' (meaning for her to taste the wine) to which she replied:

'Jesus, I wouldn't be able to open that!!'

Overheard by Anonymous, Chinese restaurant, city centre

Posted on Sunday, 28 September 2008

Close enough

Big party for the opening of a new extension at Supervalu, Balbriggan (loadsa free stuff, balloons, barbeque, etc.) in the middle of July last.

Marty Whelan is calling out numbers for the free raffle, getting increasingly frustrated as many people have left the store and therefore cannot claim their prize.

Myself, my friend, loads of other children and throngs of middle-aged women crowding around Marty, anxious to win a Supervalu hamper.

Marty: 'Our next number is 426, 426 ... anyone?'

Me (desperate for some free stuff): 'Will you take 486 instead?'

Marty: 'You know what, for sheer brass neck, yes I will!'

WHAT A LEGEND! Much to the amusement and annoyance of some, I claimed a prize. Some days later an enormous hamper of yogurts, cheese and fresh cream came to my door.

Moral of the story? Ask for free stuff and you shall receive free stuff ... and Marty Whelan is probably the nicest man on earth!

Overheard by Sarah, Supervalu Balbriggan
Posted on Saturday, 27 September 2008

Don't forget your manners!

I was visiting my cousin in Seattle last summer and we (my cousin, her husband and seven children) were all sitting down for dinner. One of the children said to me: 'Um ... can you get me some juice?'

I poured the juice and said: 'Is there something you're forgetting?'

She said: 'Um ...'

So I said: 'I'll give you a clue, it begins with "t" and ends with "hanks."'

My cousin's husband cut in and said: 'Eh ... Tom Hanks?'

Overheard by Jessica, Seattle
Posted on Friday, 26 September 2008

Wheelchair wit

I was walking my dog one day when I saw a neighbour of mine who was in a wheelchair. He had just pulled into his driveway and was attempting to get out of his car and into his wheelchair. On seeing this I thought I'd be helpful and shouted over to him:

'Hey Mick, do ye want a hand?'

To which Mick sharply replied at the top of his voice: 'No, yer all right, it's a pair of legs I want.'

Overheard by Aaron, Bayside, Dublin 13
Posted on Tuesday, 23 September 2008

White wedding

While standing in a queue in Dunnes Stores, I overheard two women talking about a wedding.

One said: 'Ah jaysus, she was gorgeous, you should have seen her dress, it was jet white.'

Overheard by Anonymous, Dunnes Stores, The Square
Posted on Monday, 22 September 2008

A slight mix-up

I was on the no. 10 bus. We reached O'Connell Street heading towards Phoenix Park when a group of about ten Spanish students got on the bus after having a conversation with the driver (who was a pure Dub) in broken Spanish. Bus pulls up at Phoenix Park and I'm behind the students getting off.

Spanish students looking lost ask: 'So, where is DCU?'

Bus driver replies: 'Ah, I taught you said da Zoooooo!'

Whole bus cracks up!

Overheard by Armagh, no. 10 bus
Posted on Monday, 22 September 2008

Fruit and veg

Guy walks up to the check-out in Tesco with a lime and hands it to the cashier. Cashier looking bemused shouts over to one of his colleagues:

'Here Johno, how much are these watermelonz?'

Overheard by Gerry, Tesco, Dundrum
Posted on Friday, 19 September 2008

Stoned

Few years ago in my car with my brother, listening to the Adrian Kennedy phone-in show about driving while stoned. Typical scumbag rings up proud of the fact that he was stoned driving. Kennedy asks, 'So, you're stoned off your box driving now?'

Scumbag replies, 'Yeah I'm stoned, but I'm not stoned stoned, know whara mean, so I'm grand.'

Overheard by Quinc, radio
Posted on Friday, 19 September 2008

Helping your fellow passengers

One night a few years ago I was taking the Nitelink home on my own after a few drinks in town.

A fella a little worse for the wear gets on and sits down beside me and asks, 'Are you getting off in Blanchardstown?'

Not wanting to give him too much information, I say, 'Yeah, somewhere around there.'

He replies, 'Great, then you can wake me up when we get to Castleknock, so I won't miss my stop!' and promptly falls asleep.

Overheard by HK, no. 39N bus
Posted on Thursday, 18 September 2008

Things you can't say

In Tolka Park watching a match. There was a black player on the team that got taken off. The guy beside me says to his girlfriend: 'Where's da black lad gone?'

His girlfriend says in disgust: 'You can't say that!'

To which he replies: 'Well, he's not f**king orange is he?'

Overheard by Rachel, Tolka Park
Posted on Monday, 15 September 2008

The generation gap

My sister asked for a Snow Patrol CD for her birthday. My mam spent ages looking in the shop for it. Eventually she gave up looking and asked the shop assistant:

'Do you have the new Snow Plough CD?'

Overheard by Oopsy!, HMV
Posted on Monday, 15 September 2008

It's being young at heart that really matters

American couple in their late seventies get on the no. 15 bus in town. They walk up to the front seats which have 'please reserve this seat if an elderly or disabled person needs it', so the woman puts her glasses on, reads the sign out loud and says to her husband:

'Oh, these seats are for the old folks, move up a bit, we'll sit at the back.'

Overheard by Anonymous, no. 15 Bus
Posted on Saturday, 13 September 2008

What an argument!

In a schoolyard, two kids were arguing, it went like this:

Boy: 'I don't like you!'

Girl: 'Oh yeah? Well I'm always gonna like you no matter what!'

Boy: 'Well I'm not gonna talk to you, even in secondary school!'

Girl: 'But we're going to different secondary schools!'

Boy: 'Great, I'll finally be away from you!'

Girl: 'Oh yeah? I know where you live! I KNOW WHERE YOU LIVE!'

Amazingly enough, the very next day they were playing together.

Overheard by Rainbow35, school in Monkstown
Posted on Saturday, 13 September 2008

Misuse of the word pooh!

With my aunt in a very upmarket department store in town. She was looking for pyjamas and underwear for her daughter with Winnie the Pooh characters on them. After looking for a while she spots a sales assistant and asks:

'Do you have any knickers with Pooh on them?'

Overheard by Claire, upmarket department store in town
Posted on Friday, 12 September 2008

Model reply!

A rather glamorous friend who happens to be a model was visiting us last weekend. She asked my six-year-old if she would like to be a model when she grew up.

The kid wiped the smile off her face with her reply: 'No thank you. I'd rather be a lady!'

Overheard by Anonymous, at home in Rathfarnham
Posted on Thursday, 11 September 2008

City of love

Had just met up with my boyfriend in Busáras after a long separation and greeted him with a passionate kiss.

This fellow walks by and says to us:

'Jaysus, save some for tomorrah!'

Overheard by Lovestruck, Busáras
Posted on Saturday, 6 September 2008

God help the waitress

While dining in a Chinese a group of women beside us ordered spare ribs. When the ribs and finger bowls were served, one of the women at the top of her voice shouted to the waitress:

'Come 'ere, we didn't order soup!'

Overheard by john, Wong's restaurant Clontarf
Posted on Tuesday, 2 September 2008

All that's left to do

On an Aer Arann flight from Galway to Dublin. The flight attendant gave out all the emergency instructions, afterwards the burly, red-faced Connemara lad beside me said:

'Jayz lads, all that's left to do now is crash.'

Overheard by Una, Aer Arann flight from Galway to Dublin
Posted on Sunday, 31 August 2008

What can be worse than 'the drink'?

Priest at Sunday mass just finished delivering a long speech on the terrible effects that alcohol consumption has on people, when an old man from the back pipes up:

'There is only one thing worse than the drink, Father ... the thirst!'

Overheard by AEK21, at mass
Posted on Friday, 29 August 2008

He could have waited

My uncle was telling us a story about how at his school if any of the priests teaching them ever died they would have a half-day. He said: 'Der was one fella who was so old we used to call him "the walking half-day".'

Then he went on: 'But we were all actually really upset when he died.'

Someone said to him: 'Why, was he really nice?'

And my uncle replied: 'No, the fecker went and died in the summer holidays so we didn't get the day off!'

Overheard by Tomtom, at home
Posted on Monday, 25 August 2008

The early stages of road rage

Parking my car outside my ma's in Tallaght. Without looking I opened the car door. A young girl, no more than seven-years-old, who was cycling her bike had to swerve to miss the car door. She does a little speed wobble and after regaining proper control of her bike looks back at me and shouts:

'Ye f**kin' eegit!'

Overheard by Anonymous, Tallaght
Posted on Monday, 25 August 2008

Magic moment!

I thought it would be a nice idea to bring my seven-year-old along while being scanned for my baby due later in September.

Who could have predicted what her reaction would be? When the picture of the baby came up on the screen she yelled:

'Oh look! He's waving at me!'

Overheard by Anonymous, doctor's clinic, The Coombe
Posted on Wednesday, 20 August 2008

Bleeding Kids

Dublin family on holiday. Mother trying to extract info from her son about what he was up to last night. Son been vary cagey and not giving much info. Mother not getting anywhere fast, in frustration shouts out: 'It's like trying to get blood out of a bleeding stone.'

Dad listening, says laughing, 'That should be easy then.'

If looks could kill he'd be a dead man now.

Overheard by PGMorris, while on a family holiday in Cornwall
Posted on Tuesday, 19 August 2008

Lessons

A foursome is waiting at the men's tee when another foursome of ladies are hitting from the ladies' tee.

The ladies are taking their time and when finally the last one is ready to hit the ball she hacks it about 10-feet, goes over to it, hacks it another 10-feet, looks up at the men waiting and says apologetically: 'I guess all those f**king lessons I took this winter didn't help.'

One of the men immediately replies in true Dublin wit: 'No, you see that's your problem. You should have been taking golf lessons instead.'

Overheard by David, Elm Green golf club, Dublin 15

Posted on Tuesday, 19 August 2008

Ouch – can't we talk it through first?

Woman on mobile phone.

'Yeah, they say it's psychological – I feel so guilty, I've been giving out to him the whole time.'

'He keeps licking himself, it's disgusting!'

'Yeah, I'm going to get him neutered!'

Overheard by Anonymous, Butler's, Henry Street

Posted on Tuesday, 19 August 2008

Beyond last orders

In a bar and last orders had gone but thought I'd chance my arm at getting another drink. Asked the barman for a drink to which he replied: 'No, no, I finish, I finish!'

Then I heard a voice from behind me and a drunk man lifts his head off the bar and starts shouting:

'Don't mind him ... he's a lying f**ker, he's not from Finland, he's Spanish!'

Overheard by Anonymous, Bar in Howth
Posted on Thursday, 14 August 2008

Modern miss!

My sister was setting off for a game of golf fairly late the other evening. Dad told her it was stupid, they wouldn't be able to see a thing, to which she came out with:

'Sure we'll be grand! Haven't we got luminous balls!'

Overheard by Anonymous, Ballybrack
Posted on Thursday, 14 August 2008

Religion class

One day in a sleepy classroom during Religion.

Teacher: 'We will have a Religion test next Friday.'

Student: 'What happens if you fail?'

A voice at the back of the class: 'YOU GO TO HELL!'

Overheard by Anonymous, a Dublin secondary school
Posted on Wednesday, 13 August 2008

Holy haircuts

In the local barber shop a guy in his sixties, called Mickey, was getting a trim. The barber, who obviously knew him well, was making small talk as usual.

'Well Mick, how are things, how did the holliers go? Were you telling me on your last visit that you were going to Italy or somewhere like that?'

'Yeah,' says Mickey, 'Rome, great so it was.'

'Were you near the Vatican?' asks the barber. 'Did you see the Pope?'

'I did,' says Mickey, getting fed up with all the questions. 'I was talking to him and all.'

'And what did he say to you Mick?' says the barber.

Mickey replies, 'He asked me "who did that to your f**king head, Michael?" '

Laughter from us all in the barber shop queue.

Overheard by Anonymous, Barbershop on Capel Street
Posted on Friday, 8 August 2008

Wine bar

Customer: 'May I have a glass of Sauvignon Blanc, please?'

Barman (best Dublin accent): 'Would you like red or white?'

Overheard by Dick, bar in Dublin 4
Posted on Tuesday, 5 August 2008

I hope so!

Boarding a flight to Lanzarote in Dublin airport. Child of about six or seven says to mother:

'Mam, is there an airport in Lanzarote?'

Overheard by Anonymous, Dublin airport
Posted on Tuesday, 5 August 2008

Kids watch too much TV

In Dunnes paying for my shopping when I hear this in front of me.

Kid: 'Mam, can Barney come to our house? We could break him out of the telly.'

Mother: 'How would we break him out of the telly?'

Kid: 'Bob the Builder could get him out.'

Mother: 'But then the telly would blow up.'

Kid: 'Well then Fireman Sam could put it out.'

The mother had nothing left to say.

Overheard by Josey, Dunnes stores
Posted on Tuesday, 5 August 2008

In the big shmoke

I was in Starbucks and a group of girls had just got a bus up from the country, dressed in the latest D4-style.

Then one of them looks at the board and says:

'I told yis there was such a thing as a frappuccino!'

Overheard by bronwyn, Starbucks, Liffey Valley
Posted on Friday, 1 August 2008

New bra size?

Some female D4 students bitching about one of their fellow students. One says:

'That's not a bra she's wearing, it's the Dundrum Flyover.'

Overheard by seosamh, on the no. 10 bus
Posted on Tuesday, 29 July 2008

Talking through his hole

A few years ago we were out drinking with a few of our friends, and one of the lads was pissin' and moaning about the fact that, as he put it, he hadn't been able to score with the ladies for ages.

We were all putting our theories forward as to what might have been the cause of such a phenomenal drought with the opposite sex, when one of the lads said:

'You might need to get checked out for Zachary's disease!'

'Zachary's disease, what the bleedin' hell is Zachary's disease?'

'It's when your arse looks Zachary like your face.'

Overheard by Derek, The Cedars pub
Posted on Saturday, 26 July 2008

Ticket collectors

Was going through Dún Laoghaire DART Station the other day, coming up to the ticket checkers at the barriers. In front of myself was a woman with a girl about four or five. The conversation was:

'Can I've your ticket, please?'

'Yea, but can she keep her ticket? She collects them.'

'So do I,' says the ticket checker.

Overheard by Les, Dún Laoghaire DART Station

Can you imagine how the commuters feel then?

One morning on my way to work the DART was stopped outside Connolly Station. After being there for quite a while the Dub driver makes an announcement:

'Sorry for the delay, but there are no free platforms at Connolly Station. We will get going as soon as one becomes available ... I know it's wrecking me head!'

Overheard by Noodlie, Southbound DART

Posted on Wednesday, 23 July 2008

Wakey-wakey!

Overheard at a bus stop yesterday evening:

Woman #1: 'Had the most peculiar feeling all day today that it was Monday!'

Woman #2: 'It *IS* Monday.'

Woman #3: 'Ah, well, that explains it then!'

Overheard by Anonymous, bus stop, College Green

Posted on Tuesday, 22 July 2008

Spanish soup

A friend was living in San Francisco years back. A new Spanish bar had opened and he went down to investigate. He heard a loud Dublin accent in the crowd shouting:

'Hey Malachy, me Gestapo soup is cowild.'

Overheard by Paul, San Francisco 1992

Posted on Monday, 21 July 2008

Motorways, exciting?

While sitting on the wedding bus that was to bring us from Gardiner Street Church to the wedding reception in Enfield, I saw one of the posh Howth girls get on and say:

'Oooo, I'm so excited! We're going to go on the motorway!'

As someone who's been on my fair share of motorways, I can only presume she usually travels by helicopter.

Overheard by Lisa, on the wedding bus outside
Gardiner Street Church
Posted on Monday, 21 July 2008

Sandy bitch

My Polish friend asked if I could drive him to the Airport to pick up a few of his friends arriving from Poland for a holiday here. Afterwards, driving back with his friends he turned to me and said: 'John, tell my friends about the bitches in Dublin?'

A little shocked, I asked what he meant by that, and he replied: 'My friends want to go down to the bitch for a swim sometime.'

I had a little laugh before I corrected his pronunciation.

Overheard by Anonymous, in my car
Posted on Sunday, 20 July 2008

Have you no beds to go to?

Two old geezers shooting the s**t in our local, one asks the other:

Geezer #1: 'Charlie, did ya get the new bed you were telling me about?'

Geezer #2: 'Yeah, it's bleedin' luvely.'

Geezer #1: 'The manufacturer should get an Academy Award!'

Geezer #2: 'What?'

Geezer #1: 'Best Supporting Mattress!'

Geezer #2: 'Ya know Charlie? Yer a bleedin' eegit!'

Overheard by Derek, local pub
Posted on Monday, 14 July 2008

Who needs brains when you have Daddy's money?

Bunch of yummy drummies on a flight to Malaga. All about 17–18. Very cocksure on their way to Marbella, one had asked for a latte during the in-flight service! Half way through the flight one gets up to go to toilet, stands outside the door with the green sign for a few minutes, then turns to her friend two rows away and asks:

'Does vacant mean empty?'

Shows you can't buy smarts!

Overheard by Anonymous, Aer Lingus flight to Malaga
Posted on Friday, 11 July 2008

In stitches

My sister was walking down Moore Street enjoying the usual sales banter when she passed a stall where this woman was shouting out: 'Get your plasters ... five for a Euro.'

Then she looks at my sister and says: 'D'ya got any cuts luv?'

Overheard by Áine, my sister Katriona heard it on Moore Street
Posted on Thursday, 10 July 2008

Nostalgia

Overheard an aul' codger in Grogan's one evening while he was holding court with a group younger than himself.

'Nostalgia isn't what it used to be. In my grandfather's day for instance ...'

Overheard by John, Grogan's pub
Posted on Thursday, 10 July 2008

Festival madness

Walking along Grange Road beside Marley Park on the day of a concert last summer. A Dublin bus pulls up alongside me crammed with festival goers. All I heard was the driver shouting out at the top of his voice:

'If one more person asks me where Marley Park stop is, I am not going to stop and open these doors!'

Overheard by Aine, Grange Road, Rathfarnham
Posted on Thursday, 10 July 2008

Can't believe a word you hear!

Two women chatting in the supermarket:

Woman #1: 'Wasn't it awful the way Floyd was killed off with an injection on Fair City last night!'

Woman #2: 'Couldn't tell you – I never watch it.'

Woman #1: 'Same here. Haven't seen it for years! It's awful rubbish!'

Overheard by Anonymous, in Tesco, Clondalkin
Posted on Tuesday, 8 July 2008

Caring cleaning lady

While in the Rotunda with my wife, a foreign lady in the same ward mistook a cleaning lady for a nurse and asked her if she could go to the toilet even though she was still hooked up to a drip. The cleaning lady replied, 'You can do what ya bleedin' want.'

As the lady struggled her way to the toilet the cleaner turns to the rest of the ward and in her finest Dublin accent announces:

'Someone should tell her it's pregnant she is ... not f**kin' paralysed!'

Overheard by Vinny, Rotunda Hospital
Posted on Monday, 7 July 2008

Confused commuter

At a ticket desk in Heuston a guy says: 'Can I have a return ticket, please?'

'Where to?'

'Back here.'

Overheard by Shane, Heuston Station
Posted on Saturday, 5 July 2008

Ah, now that's a bit racist!

Outside Alex's Newsagent, when I overheard a woman saying to some bloke: 'It's open all night, is it?'

His reply was: 'Sure, they're Chinese, they don't sleep!'

Overheard by Eggster, Outside Alex's Newsagent, Dun Laoghaire
Posted on Friday, 4 July 2008

Time warp

Heuston Station, Fastrack area.

Man with parcel says, 'When's the next train to Kilkenny?'

Man behind counter says, 'You just missed it.'

Overheard by Anto, Fastrack, Heuston Station
Posted on Friday, 4 July 2008

Space invader

In a Temple Bar pub recently I overheard the following.

Wannabe posh girl with an indistinguishable accent (dort, mid-Atlantic) says to a local who seemed to be pestering her.

'You're invading my space.'

To which he replied, 'Why don't you close your mouth, you might free up some.'

Overheard by Leviathan, Temple Bar
Posted on Thursday, 3 July 2008

Not the brightest

Currently sharing a house with a few people. A few months ago, one of the lads came into the sitting room and informed us that 'the fuse in the light switch for the bathroom was gone!'

Took him a while to figure out that it was, in fact, the light bulb that was gone.

Overheard by Fionn, at home
Posted on Wednesday, 2 July 2008

Doggy fare

While on a bus recently I noticed this young lad standing at the bus stop with his dog as the bus was pulling in. He stepped on, obviously presuming the dog would go home, put his money in and continued to proceed upstairs.

All of a sudden the bus driver screams, 'Oi, get off my bus!' The young lad, presuming it was him comes back down looking confused. He sees the dog sitting at the bottom of the stairs, wagging his tail and starts roaring laughing.

The bus driver who was not amused asks him what's so funny and quick as you like the young lad turns around and goes, 'Wha? Did he not pay his fare?!'

He gets the dog off the bus and runs back upstairs with a smile on his face. Gave everyone a good laugh.

Overheard by Christian, Dublin no. 150 bus
Posted on Wednesday, 2 July 2008

In a league of their own

Two apprentices reading their morning paper on the Luas when one turns to the other and says:

'See two Irish lads are joining Serie B. They're a massive Italian club!!'

Overheard by Fionn, Red line, Luas
Posted on Wednesday, 2 July 2008

True Dub wit — the oldies are the best!

Waiting with a friend in the queue for an ATM. Lady in her thirties was spending a lot of time at the machine. Dub man in his late seventies/ eighties behind her getting increasingly agitated blurts out:

'Ya know, it's a bank machine not a bleedin' television!'

Overheard by Tadhg, at ATM, Grafton Street
Posted on Tuesday, 1 July 2008

The innocence of kids

Was visiting my sister and nephew, who was four at the time. My sister was planning her second child and the little fella kept asking for a baby brother. So, after trying to fob him off, she said to him in true Catholic style, 'Ask holy God for a baby and we might get one.'

In response the cute little fecker replied, 'But mam, don't be silly, my belly is too small for a baby, he'll have to put it in yours!'

The innocence of it all ...

Overheard by Anonymous, Kildare
Posted on Tuesday, 1 July 2008

The recession has begun

More seen than heard.

I was in Mace buying some Lucozade Sport and I spotted a new 25% extra free bottle. I checked the prices of the bottles and guess what it said?

Lucozade Sport: €1.99

Lucozade Sport 25% extra free: €2.50?????

Overheard by Mike, Mace
Posted on Tuesday, 1 July 2008

Being invited for drinks by a D4-head

While having a smoke with my mate outside the Front Lounge on Parliament Street, there was this D4-head on his mobile pacing back and forth in front of us when all of a sudden we hear him say in this ever-so-grand D4 accent:

'Oh myself and Ian are drinking up a storm in the Front Lounge, you simply must come and join us!'

Overheard by Donnie, Front Lounge Bar
Posted on Monday, 30 June 2008

A little white lie!

A friend of mine got fed up being nagged by her kid to run out and buy ice cream from those musical whippy vans that she told him:

'When you hear the music, it means their ice cream is all gone!'

It seems to be working so far ...

Overheard by Anonymous, friend's house, Raheny
Posted on Sunday, 29 June 2008

What time is it?

Working nights as a garda in an inner city Garda station. One night I spent most of my time looking after a particularly drunk man who had been arrested.

He was in the cell and wanted to ring his girlfriend to tell her he had been arrested, I duly obliged and gave him use of a phone, he rang her and obviously woke her up. She asked him what time it was.

To which he replied, with a very grand sweep of the arm: 'It's all hours of the morning!'

Overheard by Anonymous, work
Posted on Friday, 27 June 2008

American presidential election

At a party a few months back there was a gang discussing the American elections and who their preferred choices for president were, some mentioning McCain, others mentioning Obama. One guy, who had been silent up to this, says,

'I don't know much about them lads, I just really hope Hillary Duff gets it.'

Overheard by Spuds, my 21st party, Dublin
Posted on Tuesday, 24 June 2008

You can never have too much protection

I was going on summer holidays with my girlfriend and we were packing our bags when she turns around to me and says,

'Make sure to pack sun cream, you need your UVF protection.'

Overheard by B-Dogg, at home
Posted on Sunday, 22 June 2008

Spot the difference!

A friend's seven-year-old, being driven through the city during the referendum campaign, wanted to know:

'Da, are you voting for the politicians or the monkeys?'

Overheard by Anonymous, friend's car, Dublin city
Posted on Sunday, 22 June 2008

Keeping her options open ...

My husband reminded me of this conversation he overheard between myself and a home-help 'treasure' I had some years ago, at a time when hand-me-downs were always welcomed:

'Mary, what size shoes do you wear?'

'Oh, anything between 4 and 9, Mrs ...'

Overheard by Anonymous, domesticity in my
home some time ago
Posted on Saturday, 21 June 2008

Dialectically Dublin

Having a post-English language exam drink with students in a pub in Temple Bar, a pair of ethnic

Dubs muscled in on the conversation.

'What are yiz doing here?' says one.

I explained that the students had just finished an English language exam. 'Jayzus, YIZ are in the right place to learn English,' says the other.

'Why is that?' enquired one of the students.

'The best English in the world is SPOKE in Dublin.'

'That's a lofty claim,' quips another student, 'how can you be so sure?'

'I SEEN it WROTE somewhere.'

Overheard by Mark, The Auld Dubliner
Posted on Friday, 20 June 2008

Musical mix-up

I was in the now defunct Music City CD store in Dún Laoghaire about five years ago. I was looking under the 'C' section for a CD. There was a guy beside me rifling his way through the 'D' section in vain. He turned to me and said in an exasperated voice:

'D'ya know where I can find Deagles?' (The Eagles)

And he was serious ...

Overheard by Jamie, Record Shop, Dún Laoghaire
Posted on Thursday, 19 June 2008

Great place altogether

I was passing the GPO in town and these two American girls were walking by, I hear one of them saying:

'What does G-P-O stand for?'

To which the other replies:

'Oh, someone told me earlier on that it stood for Great Place Altogether, strange way the Irish spell, isn't it?'

Overheard by Anonymous, outside the GPO
Posted on Wednesday, 18 June 2008

She's doing really well ...

My mam was telling me and my brother about a girl we used to know.

'She's doing really well for herself ... sure, she's driving a Lanzarote.'

Overheard by Louie, at home
Posted on Wednesday, 18 June 2008

Have a cuppa

Was in Lemongrass last week with my mam, broadening her horizons (she always eats in the same places). After dinner she was stuffed, but I was ordering a coffee and advised her to have an espresso, she had never had one before. On her first taste she said:

'Jaysus ... you could chew that!'

Overheard by Big Al, Lemongrass
Posted on Tuesday, 17 June 2008

Tasty!

On a Friday night, two years ago, I was getting a taxi from Monkstown into Harcourt Street. There were four excited lads in the taxi and our taxi man was in flying form. He got especially vocal as we approached Wesley junior disco in

Donnybrook. With no encouragement from us, he rolled down the window and shouted:

'Love the furry boots darlin'!!' before turning to us and saying in total honesty,

'Jesus, if ya melted that skirt off her I'd have it in me next burger!'

Disgusting but enough to send us into hysterics!

Overheard by Anonymous, Dublin taxi in Donnybrook
Posted on Friday, 13 June 2008

Stick it in

I was in the queue in McDonald's and the couple ahead were ordering their food. When it came to payment they chose to pay with a credit card. The man working the till turned to the woman and said:

'Just stick it in down de bottom there.'

To which the woman's boyfriend replied:

'Jaysus, you're very forward, aren't ya?'

Overheard by Anonymous, McDonald's, Blanchardstown
Posted on Thursday, 12 June 2008

What would you do?

I overheard a conversation between two of my friends in a bar in town.

Mossy: 'Si, what would you do if you saw twenty euro in a urine-soaked toilet?'

Si: 'Probably pick it out, why, where is it?'

Mossy: 'In my pocket!'

Overheard by Anonymous, Temple Bar
Posted on Wednesday, 11 June 2008

An insult or a compliment?

Recently bought a fabulous digital camera at Aldi for a bargain €199. I'm still learning all the tricks – deleting, transferring to computer, short videos – the works. I brought it to the local fête last Sunday, snapping all and sundry. One elderly lady politely asked for a copy of the photo when they 'came out', at which point I was able to click a few buttons and show her the photo already on the screen.

She was astonished and asked, 'Where did you buy it? How much was it?'

I heard myself say, 'One ninety-nine in Aldi.'

'You'd never guess,' she gasped, 'I'm sure it's JUST as good as the others!'

Overheard by Anonymous, Garden fête, Clonsilla
Posted on Wednesday, 11 June 2008

He's (not) got a ticket to ride

After the Bon Jovi concert last night in Punchestown, we were getting a Dublin bus home. I had just got on and I was waiting for my boyfriend at the driver's door. The bus driver stopped two lads who were trying to get on.

Bus driver: 'Show me your tickets lads.'

Lad #1: 'Here's me ticket.'

Bus driver: 'That's your concert ticket, you're not getting on with that.'

Lad #2: 'Well, what other ticket do you want?'

Bus driver: 'Your bus ticket, ya plank.'

Was probably going to be a long walk home for them!

Overheard by Yvonne, Bon Jovi concert,
Punchestown, Co. Kildare
Posted on Sunday, 8 June 2008

Rod Stewart eat your heart out

A mate of mine turned to some gorgeous blonde girl last night, whose head was so far up her arse she could lick her belly button from the inside, and said:

'You look like that famous singer.'

Girl turns with a big smile: 'Oh yeah?'

Mate: 'Yeh the blonde one.'

Girl (still all smiles): 'Who?'

Mate: 'Rod Stewart.'

Overheard by Charlo, Sin nightclub
Posted on Saturday, 7 June 2008

D4s — up their own bloody arses!

'So, loike, I'm gonna loike scoosh around to DBF for some JPBs loike, uh, you wanna scoosh along?'

Translation: 'I'm going to Donnybrook Fair to get a pack of John Player Blues, would you like to come?'

Overheard by Anonymous, Donnybrook
Posted on Saturday, 7 June 2008

When in Rome

Just after the new Pope was instated my sister and her boyfriend were visiting Rome for the weekend. They were in a queue to go to a mass being said by the new Pope.

While in the queue my mother sent her a text asking her to 'say hello to Ratzinger for me'.

Not realising that this was the real name of the new Pope my sister looked at the text and said loudly to her boyfriend:

'What's a Ratzinger?'

Cue lots of looks and laughter from devout Catholics.

Overheard by J, Rome
Posted on Friday, 6 June 2008

Abstract thinking

Standing in the corridor of my school and two lads were standing nearby talking about smoking hash.

Guy #1: 'I tell ya, it cost me a fair bit this time but, man, it was worth it.'

Guy #2: 'Yeah, I'm gonna get some this weekend. I haven't done it in ages. I'm startin' to miss out on the buzz.'

The second fella goes on for a while in a loud voice when, suddenly, the principal rounds the corner and the first lad notices and tries to make it look like they weren't talking about hash, and he says:

'You know I was never a massive fan of Picasso, but as the years went on and he started to get weirder with his design he began to appeal to me.'

Quick thinking for a hash smoker.

Overheard by B-Dogg, school corridor
Posted on Friday, 6 June 2008

Ready! Steady! Go!

One lovely day out in the back garden, me and my girlfriend Claire were watching a flock of racing pigeons fly around.

She had never seen them before and asks, 'Why are those pigeons flying around in a circle?'

I explain that they were racing pigeons flying around their coop.

Then she asks me, 'So, how do you know which one is winning?'

Overheard by Karl, Crumlin
Posted on Friday, 6 June 2008

The basement is in the basement!

In a famous Irish department store on Henry Street we get asked the same question every single bleedin' day, but today was even worse:

Old dear: 'Excuse me, where is the bargain basement?'

Assistant: 'In the basement.'

Old dear: 'Oh really? I thought it was on the top floor.'

Assistant: 'No Madam, the bargain basement has always been in the basement.'

Overheard by Accessories Babe, Arnotts
Posted on Tuesday, 3 June 2008

What you'd call mastering the Irish sense of humour?

On the train pulling into Dublin after a weekend of side-splitting banter and messing on a stag in Galway. The stag turns round to his Asian work mate, who has lived in Ireland for over six years now and has adopted a great knack for the Irish turn of phrase, and says,

'Jaysus, Tarang you're some cowboy.'

To which Tarang replies, 'No my friend, I'm some Indian.'

Overheard by Anonymous, on the train
Posted on Tuesday, 3 June 2008

Overcoming procrastination

Friend talking about her effort (or lack of) to motivate herself:

'I even bought a book on overcoming procrastination but have procrastinated on reading it!'

Overheard by AEK21, TCD
Posted on Tuesday, 3 June 2008

The irony!

Not so much what I heard as what I saw.

Driving down to Greystones from Bray and the usual posters all over the poles and fences telling us to 'Vote YES' and the odd one telling us to 'Vote NO'. Well, on one pole you have a poster by Dick Roche urging us to 'Vote Yes for Ireland and for Europe', and just above it on the same pole you have a poster saying 'The Greatest European Circus'.

Now that about sums up the Lisbon Treaty courtesy of Dick and the circus.

Overheard by Anonymous, driving down to Greystones from Bray
Posted on Monday, 2 June 2008

Working-class honesty

Was at a wedding recently and was sitting beside what I initially viewed as a 'skobie' bloke to my left and a 'lady' (as she kept reminding the table) to my right. He was drinking bottles of Bud and the lady was drinking sparkling water.

When it came to the toast the bride and groom sent the waiters around to ask the attendees what they would like to drink for the toast. At this moment the skobie went to the toilet. Upon his return the 'lady' next to him informed him that the bride and groom were buying a drink for the toast.

He said: 'Ah sure, the poor f**kers are gonna need all the poke they have, I just want a bottle of Bud luv, but wait 'n' ye see all the hungry feckers ordering brandy and gingers.'

Guess what the 'lady' ordered?

Overheard by The Stork, at a Wedding
Posted on Sunday, 1 June 2008

Where are ya?

Guy speaking loudly on his phone in a strong Dublin accent.

'Where are ya?'

Pause.

'What are ya doing in Singapore?'

Pause.

'Oh, Inchicore!'

Overheard by kev, O'Connell Street
Posted on Saturday, 1 June 2008

Out of the mouths of babes ...

My nine-year-old granddaughter passed through the kitchen while I was listening to the news the other day.

'I don't know why you listen to her,' she commented, 'all she does is complain!'

Overheard by Anonymous, Laurel Park, Clondalkin

Posted on Saturday, 31 May 2008

In a bit of a stew!

The checkout girl was serving her husband who was in front of me in the supermarket. Just before he left she said to him:

'Will you peel the cauli so's it's ready when I get home?'

He looked a bit puzzled, and said 'peel the cauli ...?'

'Ah forget it!' she said, 'You'll probably only do the same thing you did to the carrots!'

Overheard by Anonymous, Superquinn, Lucan

Posted on Saturday, 31 May 2008

Randy Eamonn

In a TV store one afternoon. An elderly well-to-do woman came in saying she had tried to sign up directly with Sky, but they wouldn't put the satellite dish on her chimney because the installers weren't insured to go higher than 12-feet off the ground. The shop assistant wrote down his local installer's phone number and said:

'Sure, give Eamonn a ring, he'd get up on anything.'

Overheard by Anonymous, TV Store
Posted on Friday, 30 May 2008

Thanks for the heads up

I was in the doctor's surgery one morning waiting to be seen. A young boy came in with his mother for vaccinations. He was smiling and happy, completely oblivious to what was about to happen. He emerged after seeing the doctor with tears streaming down his face and was very upset.

The doctor then came back out to the waiting room to call in his next patient, a man in his twenties. Seeing this, the boy decided it was his duty to warn this man and save him from a similar fate. He yelled 'wait' and ran over to the man. He then whispered to him, 'Look out, he's a doctor!'

The guy couldn't stop laughing but thanked him for the heads up.

Overheard by Aoife, doctor's surgery
Posted on Friday, 30 May 2008

Role models

So, there I am walking down the road after getting off my bus when I passed three kids – who all looked about five or six – playing a game of football. The one between the jumpers (obviously the keeper) shouts to one of the other boys:

'Hey Mikey, who are you playin' as?'

Without missing a beat the kid jumps on the ground and looks up and shouts back: 'Can't ya see I'm Drogba?!'

Overheard by Coffey, Skerries
Posted on Thursday, 29 May 2008

Sex and the City – should come with a health warning

Three girls on the bus discussing the *Sex and the City* film, one of them had obviously been to see it.

Girl: 'I loved it, I was dying for a pee but wouldn't go in case I'd miss it and [lowered her voice here but I craned my ears!] I peed myself a little when I was laughing! Sinead wouldn't look at me all night after it!'

Overheard by Anonymous, no. 16A bus
Posted on Thursday, 29 May 2008

You don't need a ticket for this Trinity Ball

American tourist in front of the golden sphere-shaped sculpture outside the Berkeley Library in Trinity College.

'Is this the Trinity Ball?'

Overheard by AEK21, Berkeley Library, Trinity College
Posted on Wednesday, 28 May 2008

Gianni Walker fashion victim

A few years back, we found ourselves waiting for a friend in the emergency room at Beaumont Hospital on a Friday night. This drunk gets seated beside us with blood all over the front of his white t-shirt. He looks over at us, smiles while stretching out his shirt and says:

'Check it out, it's a VERSACE!'

Overheard by Skilaro, Beaumont Hospital
Posted on Wednesday, 28 May 2008

Pimp my bollox

Seen not heard.

A '98 Silver Passat in Finglas, go faster stripes, fancy lights with the word 'BOLLOX' done in really fancy silver letters screwed in just above the reg. And just in case the gardaí weren't sure whether to stop and search this vehicle, a really fancy cannabis leaf also in silver attached to the back ...

Overheard by Anonymous, Finglas
Posted on Tuesday, 27 May 2008

The lesser of two evils

Two teenage girls at the back of the no. 11 bus this morning.

Girl #1: 'I can't believe you believed her, you're feckin' thick.'

Girl #2: 'Shut up Megan, you thought George Clooney was president of America.'

Overheard by Alan, no. 11A bus

Posted on Tuesday, 27 May 2008

Festival fashion

In Oxegen last year, walking around in the rain and mud, everyone scattering for shelter. Spot some dude wearing what looked like an abandoned tent fashioned into a jacket.

My mate says, in a jokey way, 'Is that a tent ur wearing!?'

Guy replies, with a look of absolute disgust on his face, 'No, it's a gazebo.'

And swaggers off.

Overheard by Brian, Oxegen 2007

Posted on Monday, 26 May 2008

Sweet as rain!

Walking through Meath Street one day just as it started to rain. As I was passing two women, one says, 'Ah jaysus, here's the rain!'

To which the other woman replies, 'Ah relax Margaret, you're not made of sugar so ya wont melt!'

Overheard by Superred, Meath Street

Posted on Sunday, 25 May 2008

Ah bless 'em nurses

We were reminiscing on being student nurses when one piped up about being in third year and being assigned to do work experience in A&E, Tallaght.

A young man was brought in with a gunshot wound to the lower leg and was surrounded by all medical personnel. This is when they thought it would be a perfect opportunity for her as a student nurse to assess his pain status. Bravely, she approached him knowing that all eyes were on her and asked him how his pain was. 'Well it's pretty bad,' he said.

'Okay. Can you describe it to me? Is it a shooting pain?'

Even the young victim broke out laughing with the doctors. She on the other hand went puce, turned around and walked out of the room.

Overheard by Anonymous, Pavilion Bar, Trinity College
Posted on Friday, 23 May 2008

Are those fake eyelashes?

At the top of the stairs in the science building in DCU. Two women were having a conversation. One complimented the other.

'Ah, sure, you could sweep the floor with those eyelashes!'

Overheard by Anonymous, science building, DCU
Posted on Wednesday, 21 May 2008

No brainer

At a poker night a few weeks ago and there was an argument going on about who was the worst ever foreigner in the Premier League.

Some bloke says, 'Definitely Djibril Cisse, he was even sh**e on a *Question of Sport*.'

Overheard by Anonymous, Racecourse Inn
Posted on Tuesday, 20 May 2008

Italian literature

Two girls were sitting in front of me on the Luas talking about a fellow student.

Girl #1: 'Yeah, she's, like, really smart, she has a degree in Italian Literature.'

Girl #2: 'Italian Literature?'

Girl #1: 'Yeah, you know like Dante's Inferno and stuff.'

Girl #2: 'Oh, Dante's Inferno. Okay. So who wrote that?'

Girl #1: 'I can't remember!'

Overheard by Anonymous, Luas to Heuston
Posted on Tuesday, 20 May 2008

One in a million

Was in Keating's on Store Street about 25 years ago having an early pint with me Da. A very drunk aul' fella ordered a pint.

Barman: 'Yuv had enough! I'm not servin' ya anymore.'

As the aul' fella staggered out, he quipped, 'Sure you've only got one pub! I've got millions!'

Overheard by P, Keating's
Posted on Tuesday, 20 May 2008

Spiritual toilet humour

One of the lads in my office comes back in from the toilet. Other lad leaves his desk and heads to the toilet. Comes back a minute later with a look of disgust on his face and says to the first lad,

'Ahh for f**ks sake, Damo, you should be goin'
to confession after what you did in there.'

Overheard by Anonymous, in work
Posted on Monday, 19 May 2008

Vintage Dublin wit

I was having a quick pint in a pub on
Marlborough Street and I heard a few aul' lads
telling stories about their mothers, when one
said:

'I remember when I was around seven, I seen a
lovely bike in a shop window and I went home
and said to me Ma, "Ma, there's a lovely bike in
Grenville's shop window," and she said, "How
much is it son?" and I said, "Two-and-six, Ma"
then she said to me, "Do you want it son?" and I
said, "yeah Ma", then she said, "Well, son, you
go back down to the shop and keep your eye on
it ... cause your arse is never going to get
anywhere near it!"'

Overheard by Graham, pub on Marlborough Street
Posted on Sunday, 18 May 2008

Mission impossible!

My next-door-neighbour and I were discussing
the fun we get from our grandchildren one day
when he said:

'We enjoy them so much, we should have had
them first!'

Overheard by Anonymous, over the garden gate, Lucan
Posted on Friday, 16 May 2008

The innocence of it all

I was coming down the escalator in Marks and Spencer's on Henry Street a few weeks ago. There was a woman and her little girl behind me and she said to her mam:

'Why won't granny and granddad have a baby?'

Overheard by Megan, Marks and Spencer, Henry Street
Posted on Thursday, 15 May 2008

The five-year-old philosopher

My boyfriend was playing with his five-year-old nephew the other day when the conversation took a turn to the philosophical.

Nephew: 'Didn't God build everything?'

Boyfriend agreed.

Nephew: 'So aren't builders great then doing that for God?'

Boyfriend agreed.

Nephew: 'Didn't God make all the people as well?'

Boyfriend agreed again ...

Nephew: 'Even English people?'

Overheard by butterfly, at home
Posted on Wednesday, 14 May 2008